The Catskills
Farm to Table
Cookbook

COURTNEY WADE

Hatherleigh Press is committed to preserving and protecting the natural resources of the earth. Environmentally responsible and sustainable practices are embraced within the company's mission statement.

Visit us at www.hatherleighpress.com and register online for free offers, discounts, special events, and more.

The Catskills Farm to Table Cookbook

Library of Congress Cataloging-in-Publication Data is available.

ISBN: 978-1-57826-842-9

Printed in the United States

10 9 8 7 6 5 4 3 2 1

Contents

Introduction

I LIKE TO KNOW where my food comes from. Not in the broad sense of which grocery store were my items picked up at—actually knowing *where* my food comes from.

Growing up on a farm in a small town in the Catskill Mountains of upstate New York, the concept of food traceability was instilled in me at an early age. Some may call it being picky, finicky, or even snobby, but I've embraced this quality in myself. Knowing where the meat and vegetables on my plate originated from, along with the methods with which it was grown, harvested, and prepared, are things that everyone should care about.

The term 'farm to table' refers to an environment and nutrition-based movement that promotes local, healthier, and pure food products, as opposed to those that are processed. The goal of the farm to table movement is to connect individuals with the natural world by allowing them to understand and see where their food comes from.

The farm to table movement naturally promotes community involvement, too—when someone cares about where their food is coming from, they also want to know the farmer or producer responsible for it. And this is where the Catskills really shine, with farms throughout the region offering farm tours and hands-on learning and restaurants featuring as many locally sourced products as they can, promoting seasonal eating. Small breweries and distilleries are opening with unique offerings utilizing ingredients found locally, while summertime farmers markets make accessing these valued goods easier than ever. Recently there seems to be more than one in every town!

All this is because the Catskills offer everything needed to actively participate in this movement, which has now become a way of life. From plentiful land to grow vegetables and graze livestock, rivers and streams for fishing, and forest for wild game and foraging, those who look to embrace a more mindful and engaged way of eating find endless opportunities waiting for them in the Catskill Mountains.

THE CATSKILLS
New York

This cookbook is your guide as you roam about the Catskills, offering recipes to take you through the seasons of upstate New York. Fresh vegetables and fruit, meat, dairy, wild game and foraged produce all take center stage, because that is what eating in the Catskills is all about. The hardworking farms and restaurants that emphasize the use of local goods and produce year-round are also featured, providing a tour of the farm to table movement in the Catskills.

Knowing what goes into the food on your plate is not a trend or a fad—it's a renewed understanding of the processes, the time, the individuals, the community, and the lifestyle behind it all.

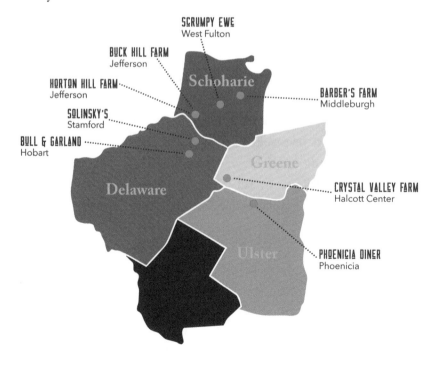

SCRUMPY EWE
West Fulton

BUCK HILL FARM
Jefferson

HORTON HILL FARM
Jefferson

SOLINSKY'S
Stamford

BULL & GARLAND
Hobart

Schoharie

BARBER'S FARM
Middleburgh

Greene

Delaware

CRYSTAL VALLEY FARM
Halcott Center

Ulster

PHOENICIA DINER
Phoenicia

The Catskills Farm to Table Cookbook

Spring

Nettle Soup

SERVES 8

Stinging nettles were one of the first wild plants that I learned to forage for. I like to use them in place of spinach in recipes; just be sure to steam or blanch them to get rid of the stingers.

SOUP

2 tablespoons butter

1 small onion, finely chopped

1 pound white potatoes, peeled and cubed

8 cups chicken stock (see page 192 for recipe)

1 large bunch stinging nettles

1 cup heavy cream

Salt and pepper, to taste

CROUTONS

6 slices peasant bread

Olive oil

Garlic powder

Salt and pepper, to taste

Melt butter in a heavy stockpot over medium heat. Stir in the onions and cook until soft and fragrant, about 4 minutes. Add potatoes and stock and cover until potatoes fall apart with a fork, about 30 minutes.

While potatoes cook, remove stems from nettles while wearing gloves. Discard the stems and place leaves in a bowl.

Once the potatoes are cooked, add the leaves to the pot, cover, and cook for 8 to 10 minutes until completely wilted. Turn off the heat and puree soup in blender when cooled, or use an immersion blender until smooth. Stir in cream and season with salt and pepper to taste.

Cube bread and spread out on a baking sheet. Drizzle with olive oil and season with salt, pepper, and garlic powder. Broil on high until browned and crispy.

Sprinkle croutons on soup when ready to serve.

> **COOK'S NOTE:** When harvesting nettles, wear gloves and clip the top leaves of the plant with scissors to avoid contact with the stingers.

Pasta with Ramps

SERVES 4

This was the dish that I came up with when I first found a patch of ramps, primarily because the patch only had about twenty ramps in total! Lightly charring the ramps gives them a kind of toasty flavor that adds another level of depth to this simple dish.

1 pound thin spaghetti

1 bunch of ramps (10)

2 tablespoons olive oil

Salt and pepper, to taste

In a large pot, cook pasta in boiling salted water, stirring occasionally, until pasta is al dente.

Meanwhile, lightly oil a grill pan heated to medium-high heat. Lay ramps in batches on the pan and cook until greens become wilted. Coarsely chop greens of the cooked ramps and finely chop the bulb.

Drain pasta, reserving 1½ cups of the pasta water. Add olive oil to the pot and add chopped ramps. Return pasta to pot and toss. Add reserved pasta water and season with salt and pepper. Cook until glossy and pasta is well coated.

COOK'S NOTE: When harvesting ramps, be sure not to dig up the entire root system of the plant to ensure that they grow back the following season.

BUCK HILL FARM

JEFFERSON, NY

I F YOU LIVE in the small town of Jefferson, New York, you know that the best place for breakfast on the weekends is at Buck Hill Farm. Vehicles of locals and visitors alike will quickly fill the driveway and line both sides of the road on Saturday and Sunday mornings.

Buck Hill Farm was originally owned and operated by Charles and Lynn Buck, who quickly established high standards by producing consistently good maple syrup the most efficient way they knew how. Buck Hill Farm became one of the first farms to market their products at the Greenmarkets in New York City in the mid-70s, with maple syrup production steadily increasing even as the value-added product line was introduced in the 1980s.

Buck Hill Farm was purchased by Sharon, Charles and Lynn's daughter, and her husband Jeff Collins in 1993, the same year their son, Sam, was born. Incidentally, 1993 also yielded the largest maple syrup crop to date.

Sharon and Jeff continued to grow the farm by creating a large wholesale business, servicing restaurants, farm stands, and groceries, all while still taking products to the Greenmarkets in NYC. Their daughter, Charlotte, was born in 1995, the year the sap-house kitchen was renovated and the now-renowned Saturday and Sunday breakfasts began being served. The value-added product line was also expanded to include maple granola, jams, maple roasted nuts, maple caramel popcorn, and a variety of maple pickles.

In recent years, Buck Hill's business model has been re-developed to emphasize a more sustainable practice. This included eliminating long-distance deliveries, maximizing production from the land on the farm, and locally sourcing as many supplies as possible.

As an adult, Sam has found his own passion in the ever-evolving and demanding maple syrup industry. He currently oversees both sap bush management as well as syrup production, all while keeping up with livestock care, land use, and building and machinery use. Sam is a master at making do with what's available to him, and enjoys finding a balance between innovation and tradition.

After receiving her degree in Direct Marketing at FIT NYC, Charlotte returned to the farm in 2019 and is managing new projects in fundraising, hospitality and cash crop development. While she is deeply involved in helping to enhance the farms digital presence as marketing manager, she loves to spend as much time as possible outside, and can be found helping to feed the cows or out in the woods fixing sap line during sap season. She is determined to foster healthier habits at home and in the community using her fitness training certifications. Having experienced city living, she is now convinced that Buck Hill Farm is what other people dream about.

Buck Hill Farm pioneered the farm to table concept, both through their vast offering of products as well as through their weekend breakfasts. If it isn't made, raised, grown, or collected on the farm, it is most certainly sourced locally. The eggs, bacon, sausage and ham found on the menu are all sourced from the farm; the beets, cucumbers and tomatoes used to make value-added products sold at the store are all grown on the farm; apples and berries are foraged on the farm to make applesauce and unique products like elderberry elixir and blackberry tonic.

It doesn't matter if it is the first or hundredth time, a trip to Buck Hill Farm leaves a lasting impression on all who visit, whether it's from watching how the maple syrup is made or from enjoying a Catskill's farm to table breakfast. There is a reason why cars line up on the weekends, even on a back road in a small town in the Catskills: "You're not going out for breakfast; you're coming over for breakfast."

Maple Cream Pie

SERVES 12

Sharon and I wanted to feature as many Buck Hill Farm products as possible with this recipe. With its unique color and taste, the buckwheat crust is like no other pastry—and is naturally gluten-free.

CRUST

1 cup buckwheat pancake flour

⅓ cup lard

⅓ cup cold water

FILLING

¾ cup granulated maple sugar

3 tablespoons cornstarch

3 cups whole milk

4 egg yolks, beaten

1 tablespoon butter

1 teaspoon vanilla

MAPLE MERINGUE

4 egg whites

1 cup granulated maple sugar

1 teaspoon cream of tartar

Preheat oven to 375°F. To make the crust, combine pancake flour and lard in a food processor until crumbly. Add water and combine until dough forms in a ball. "Flour" your hands with the pancake mix and press dough into a 9-inch pie pan and crimp the edge. Poke holes into the crust and bake for 30 minutes.

To make the filling, combine sugar and cornstarch in a medium saucepan. Stir in milk. Cook and stir over medium heat until mixture is thick and bubbly, and coats the back of a spoon. Remove from heat. Gradually stir in about 1 cup of hot mixture into beaten egg yolks. Return the egg mixture to the saucepan and bring to a gentle boil. Reduce heat and cook for 2 minutes longer. Remove from heat and stir in butter and vanilla.

COOK'S NOTE: To measure chilled lard, fill a measuring cup with one cup of cold water. Add lard to measuring cup until the water rises to one cup and the required amount. This recipe would make the water rise to 1⅓ cup, for example.

Pour hot filling into baked pie crust. Cover with plastic wrap and chill until filling is set or overnight.

To make the meringue, beat egg whites on high with a hand or stand mixer until white and foamy. Gradually add sugar and cream of tartar and continue to beat on high until soft peaks form. Dollop meringue on top of chilled pie to completely cover the filling. Bake at 375°F to lightly brown topping, about 7–10 minutes. Serve.

Store in the refrigerator.

Ramp Butter

YIELDS 1 CUP

This recipe, generously contributed by Sharon at Buck Hill Farm, is a seasonal favorite on their spring menu. During the research for this book, she and I spent several spring afternoons walking through the sap woods, fully equipped with five gallon pails and hand trowels, looking for the distinctive emerald green leaves of the ramp.

12 ramps

1 stick salted butter, softened

Salt and pepper, to taste

Clean and roughly chop whole ramps. Combine softened butter and ramps in a food processor. Blend until ramps are finely chopped and mixture is combined. Season with salt and pepper.

Refrigerate mixture. The butter can also be stored in the freezer.

COOK'S NOTE: The prepared butter pairs well with eggs and toast, or on top of steak.

Roasted Asparagus

SERVES 4

Roasting fresh asparagus is a great alternative to steaming, providing a different texture while still preserving their flavor. In fact, it is precisely that light crunch the tips get from roasting in the oven that makes this my preferred method of preparing asparagus. Fresh ground coarse black pepper and flaky sea salt, while simple ingredients, make such a difference.

2 pounds asparagus

Olive oil

Salt and pepper

Lemon

Preheat oven to 400°F. Wash and snap the bottoms off the asparagus and place flat on a baking sheet. Drizzle with olive oil and season with salt and pepper.

Bake for 25 minutes or until asparagus are tender. Finish with fresh lemon juice and zest.

COOK'S NOTE: A variety of fresh herbs, such as dill, and flavor combinations can be used in this recipe besides the ones listed.

Sautéed Fiddleheads & Asparagus

SERVES 4

Fiddleheads are commonly harvested from the ostrich fern species in New York and are sometimes available at farmer's markets and some grocery stores. They are only available for a short period of time because they are foraged, not cultivated.

4 tablespoons butter

1 pound fiddleheads, cleaned

1 bunch asparagus, chopped

1 clove garlic, minced

Juice of half lemon

Salt and pepper, to taste

Place fiddleheads and asparagus in a medium sauté pan with ¼ cup water. Cook covered over medium heat until water evaporates and fiddleheads and asparagus are softened, about 10 minutes.

When water has evaporated, add butter and let melt. Add garlic and sauté until cooked. Finish with fresh squeezed lemon juice and salt and pepper to taste.

Rhubarb Crisp Bars

MAKES 18

Rhubarb is typically the first spring crop to pop up in the Catskills. I always eagerly await its arrival so that I can start using fresh ingredients from the garden. The fruit filling of these bars can be altered depending on the season.

1 cup packed brown sugar

2 cups rolled oats

1 cup all-purpose flour

¼ cup flax seeds

1 teaspoon cinnamon

¾ cup cold butter, cut into
    ½-inch pieces

7 cups fresh rhubarb, sliced

¼ cup corn starch

¾ cup sugar

Preheat oven to 375°F. Line a 9 x 13-inch pan with foil and lightly grease. Set aside.

In a large bowl, combine brown sugar, oats, flour, flax and cinnamon until mixed. Add the butter and, with an electric mixer, mix until completely combined and butter is not visible.

Set aside 1 cup of packed mixture. Press the remaining mixture into the bottom of the prepared pan. Bake for 20 minutes, or until dry and golden brown.

Meanwhile, combine rhubarb, corn starch and sugar in a large bowl. Spread rhubarb mixture on top of baked crust. Spread remaining crumble mixture over filling and press down slightly. Bake for 45 to 50 minutes or until filling is thickened and bubbly and topping is golden.

Cool bars to room temperature and chill before cutting to allow them to set. Store in the refrigerator.

Baby Greens & Vinaigrette

SERVES 4

Any combination of greens can be used for this salad, but baby greens have a fresh spring flavor profile. A variety of spring veggie toppings make this salad a perfect starter for a spring gathering. Any fresh or dried herbs can also be used in the vinaigrette.

SALAD

1 pound mixed baby
   greens (lettuce, spinach,
   arugula, beet greens,
   mustard greens)

2 spring onions, chopped

4 radishes, thinly sliced

VINAIGRETTE

¼ cup vegetable oil

¼ cup olive oil

½ cup apple cider vinegar

1 tablespoon sugar

½ teaspoon fresh chives

½ teaspoon fresh basil

½ teaspoon paprika

¼ teaspoon Dijon mustard

¼ teaspoon pepper

Wash and dry mixed greens and place in a serving bowl. Top with onions and radishes and toss.

In a mason jar or other screw-top jar, mix oils, vinegar, sugar, herbs, paprika, mustard, and pepper. Cover and shake well. Top each serving with vinaigrette.

Steamed Milkweed Greens

SERVES 4

Milkweed greens, or shoots, are the first edible stage of the milkweed plant. Due to their very mild flavor, I prefer to steam shoots rather than sauté them with lots of other ingredients that can overpower their more subtle taste. And drizzling them with your choice of vinegar goes a long way towards brightening the freshness of the greens.

1 pound milkweed shoots

2 tablespoons butter

Salt and pepper, to taste

Malt or cider vinegar

Wash milkweed and place in a steamer. Cook until tender and wilted.

Meanwhile, melt butter in a medium skillet. Remove milkweed from steamer and transfer to skillet. Toss and season with salt and pepper.

Drizzle with vinegar just before serving.

COOK'S NOTE: These greens should only be lightly steamed to preserve the vitamins that they contain.

Creamed Spring Peas

SERVES 4

While it does take a decent amount of time to pick the pea pods and shell the peas, the end result is well worth the work. Fresh peas are strongly recommended for this dish, but frozen peas can be substituted.

4 cups shelled fresh peas

1 small onion

2 tablespoons butter

1 tablespoon flour

½ teaspoon salt

Pepper, to taste

1 cup milk

In a medium saucepan, bring a small amount of salted water to a boil. Add peas and cook until tender, 5 to 10 minutes. Drain.

In a medium saucepan, cook onion in butter until tender and slightly translucent, but not browned. Stir in flour, salt, and pepper. Add milk all at once. Cook and stir until mixture is thickened and bubbly. Cook and stir for a minute more. Stir in peas and heat through.

Pickled Garlic Scapes

YIELDS 1 PINT

This is the perfect use for the surplus of garlic scapes that arrive in the spring. These can be compared to dilly beans because of their natural garlic flavor. The recipe yield can be increased depending on how many scapes are available.

½ pound garlic scapes

1 teaspoon dill seed

½ teaspoon whole peppercorns

¾ cup cider vinegar

¾ cup water

1 tablespoon pickling salt

Trim both ends of the scapes (the blossom and the hard part that forms from the original cut) and cut them into lengths that fit a jar. Place dill and peppercorns in the jar and pack in the trimmed scapes.

Combine the vinegar, water and picking salt in a saucepan and bring to a boil. Pour the hot brine over the scapes, leaving a ½-inch headspace. Remove air bubbles, adding more brine if necessary.

Wipe rim and adjust two-piece lids. Process in a boiling-water canner. Let cure one week before eating.

BARBER'S
FARM

Heirloom
Tomatoes
95

BARBER'S FARM

MIDDLEBURGH, NY

BARBER'S FARM HAS been a family-owned farming operation for more than 150 years. Located in the heart of the beautiful Schoharie Valley in Middleburgh, New York, Barber's Farm is a year-round destination.

Come mid-April, Barber's greenhouses are bursting with green, creating a true sense of springtime after what is typically a long and cold winter in the Catskills. Vegetable and flower plants fill the rows of the warm greenhouses. Anything you could want to plant in your garden can be found there, and if you cannot find it, one of the friendly and knowledgeable staff can. Barber's offers both conventional as well as many heirloom varieties of plants to grow.

Because the family has been stewards of their land for so long, they have a strong appreciation for how it should be treated to create excellent produce. The farm is committed to using Non GMO (genetically modified organisms) seeds for their vegetables and cover crops. The farm focuses heavily on crop rotation for maximized soil health which ultimately aides in the reduction of disease & insect pressure, therefore decreasing the need for chemical applications. They have implemented reduced tillage techniques which improve soil health and reduces fuel usage. They use biodegradable plastic on all of the fields of raised beds which eliminates plastic use. Barber's Farms is an IPM or Integrated Pest Management Farm. This means that they routinely scout the crops for disease and pest pressure. They treat crops only when a certain threshold of loss will be met. They plant disease resistant varieties of plants, which helps reduce chemical applications. They implement intensive crop rotation practices. The farm utilizes natural and biological controls when possible (For example, releasing Trichogramma wasps in the sweet corn, which is never sprayed with insecticides.) They hand harvest all of the produce. They also utilize many unique cultivation techniques to avoid use of chemical herbicides.

When the summer months roll around, Barber's farm stand is typically crowded with shoppers. The sweet corn from the farm is always highly anticipated, and a swarm of people will be around the bin, filling up their carts. Barber's offers a wide array of fresh produce at their stand in the summer, and will have multiple varieties

of tomatoes, greens, squash, peppers, potatoes, eggplant, just to name a few. Much of the produce can be purchased by the bushel as well for people to freeze and can. You can also come to the farm to harvest your own tomatoes, hot peppers, eggplant, peppers, and plum tomatoes, August through September.

The fall brings pumpkins, big and small, as well as corn stalks, gourds, and winter squash and apples. The farm stand becomes a popular spot for visitors passing through the area to see the fall foliage. The farm stand is still open in the winter, offering bulk potatoes as well as fresh greens that are grown in the high tunnels. The farm stand also offers a wide variety of products from other farms such as milk and ice cream, maple products, frozen meat, and cheeses, year-round.

Barber's Farm embodies the farm to table movement not only by offering their plants and produce, but also through their 1857 Spirits potato vodka, distilled in Middleburgh with potatoes grown on the farm. Visitors can taste the spirit right at the farm stand at their tasting room. Their love for their farm and their commitment to family has created their mission is to always improve the land, protect it, and leave it better for the future generations to come.

Grilled Asparagus & Goat Cheese Toasts

SERVES 4

A recipe crafted by my mom, featuring fresh asparagus from Barber's Farm as well as the local goat cheese that they sell at the farm stand. Any flavor of goat cheese can be used.

French baguette

10-12 asparagus stalks

Olive oil

Garlic clove

Dill

Salt and pepper, to taste

Horseradish dill goat
   cheese

Heat about 1 tablespoon of olive oil over medium-high heat in a grill pan. Arrange asparagus stalks in pan, being sure not to overlap. Cook until slightly softened and showing clear grill marks, turning once. Remove from pan and chop into bite-sized pieces. Toss with chopped, fresh dill, salt and pepper to taste, and drizzle with olive oil.

Meanwhile, slice baguette into ¾-inch slices and arrange on baking sheet. Brush with olive oil. Broil on high until lightly browned and toasted. Rub toasts with garlic clove.

Top toasts with asparagus mixture and cheese. Drizzle with olive oil.

New Potatoes with Butter & Herbs

SERVES 4

While new potatoes tend not to come in season until late June to early July, I will still argue that this is the perfect dish to accompany a spring dinner. I like to use fresh chopped parsley when I prepare them; they go well with anything that way, especially a main dish that features a sauce or gravy.

2½ pounds small new potatoes

4 tablespoons butter

2 teaspoons salt

½ teaspoon pepper to taste

3 tablespoons fresh chopped herbs (chives, parsley, dill)

In a large pot, boil potatoes in lightly salted water until just fork tender and drain. Add butter, herbs, salt, and pepper to coat the potatoes.

Strawberry Rhubarb Pie

SERVES 12

Rhubarb usually comes into season in upstate New York much earlier than strawberries, so they can be purchased early on to enjoy the rhubarb as soon as it shoots up.

ONE-CRUST PASTRY

1 cup flour

½ teaspoon salt

⅓ cup lard

2–4 tablespoons ice water

FILLING

2 cups strawberries

3 cups rhubarb, chopped

1 cup sugar

¼ cup cornstarch

1 teaspoon cinnamon

TOPPING

¾ cup flour

½ cup brown sugar

½ teaspoon cinnamon

½ cup butter

Heat oven to 400°F.

To create one-crust pastry, combine flour and salt in a medium bowl. Cut lard into flour with a pastry blender or fork, until mixture resembles coarse crumbs. Sprinkle water over flour mixture, 1 tablespoon at a time, while tossing lightly with a fork until dough is moist enough to form into a ball. Shape dough into a ball and flatten into a ½-inch thickness, rounding the edges. On a floured surface, roll lightly into an 11-inch circle. Place into a 9-inch pie pan and fold and flute edges.

For crumble topping, combine all ingredients in a medium bowl until crumbly.

For the filling, combine all ingredients and mix lightly. Spoon into pastry lined pan and top with crumble topping.

Bake pie for 45 to 60 minutes or until topping is golden brown and bubbly. Best served with whipped cream or vanilla ice cream.

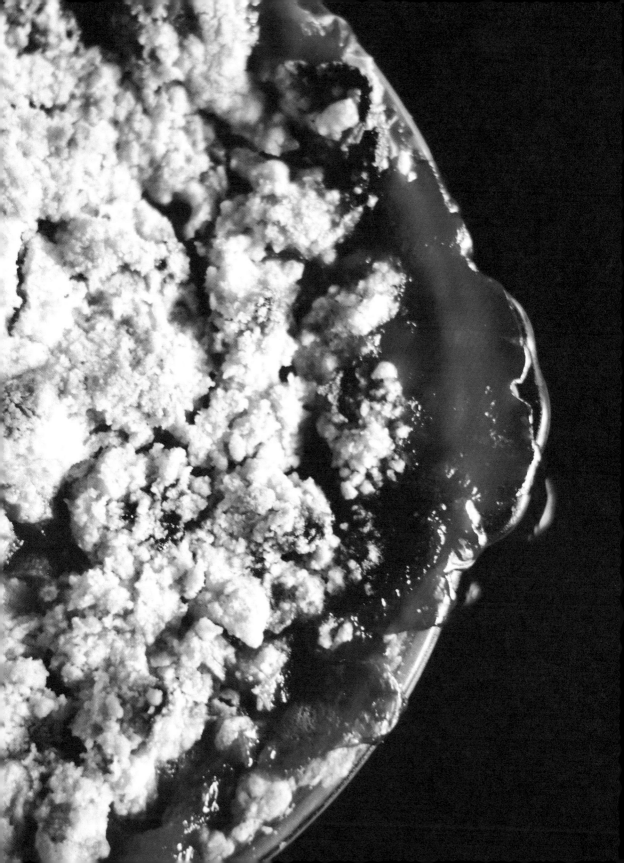

Strawberry Sweet Rolls with Mascarpone Icing

MAKES 18

The sweetness of the strawberry filling in these rolls is balanced by the coolness of the icing, which has little sugar. Enjoy for breakfast or dessert.

FILLING

1 quart strawberries, sliced

¾ cup sugar

1 teaspoon cornstarch

1 teaspoon vanilla

Cinnamon

Sugar

DOUGH

6 cups flour

½ cup sugar

2 teaspoons salt

2 packages active dry yeast

1 cup water

1 cup milk

½ cup butter

1 egg

ICING

2 cups mascarpone cheese

1 cup powdered sugar

1 teaspoon vanilla

To make filling, combine strawberries and sugar in a medium saucepan. Cook over medium heat until cooked down and softened, about 20 minutes. Add cornstarch to 1 tablespoon cold water and stir. Add to strawberry filling and stir until thickened. Remove from heat, stir in vanilla and chill.

To make the sweet roll dough, combine 2 cups flour, sugar, salt and yeast in a mixing bowl, and blend well. In a small saucepan, heat water, milk and butter until warm, around 120–130°F. Add warm liquid and egg to flour mixture. Blend on low until moistened, then beat on medium for 3 minutes. By hand, stir in 3 cups of flour until dough pulls away cleanly from sides of bowl.

On a floured surface, knead in 1 to 2 cups of flour until dough is smooth and elastic, about 8 to 10 minutes. Place dough in a greased bowl and cover loosely with plastic wrap and towel. Let dough rise in a warm place until doubled in size, about 45 to 60 minutes.

Punch down dough to remove any air pockets. Divide dough in half and shape into balls. On a floured surface, roll dough into two 12 x 12-inch squares.

Sprinkle dough with cinnamon and sugar. Spoon prepared strawberry filling over dough to coat, leaving a 1-inch gap around the edges. Roll dough and slice into 1-inch thick segments. Place sliced rolls onto greased baking dishes or cake pans, not touching each other.

Bake rolls in a 350°F oven until risen and slightly browned.

To make the icing, combine cheese, sugar and vanilla in a mixing bowl. Beat until fully blended. Frost baked rolls with icing.

Deviled Eggs

MAKES 12

Making full use of an abundant egg supply—farm fresh eggs can be found pretty much everywhere throughout the Catskills—this is the perfect appetizer for any spring event. You'll know when you have truly farm fresh eggs, as they have a much darker egg yolk compared to eggs bought from a grocery store, often to the point of being orange in color.

6 large eggs

¼ cup mayonnaise

2 tablespoons yellow mustard

1 teaspoon Worcestershire sauce

2 tablespoons ground horseradish

Salt and pepper, to taste

Paprika

Hard boil eggs. Cool and peel. Cut eggs in half lengthwise. Place yolks in bowl and mash with fork to remove large chunks. Add mayonnaise, mustard, horseradish, and Worcestershire sauce, mixing well to make a smooth mixture. Add salt and pepper to taste.

Spoon prepared filling into egg whites. Sprinkle with paprika and serve.

COOK'S NOTE: Peeling hardboiled farm fresh eggs can be a bit challenging, so using 1–2 week old eggs for this recipe is recommended.

Spring Pea Soup

SERVES 8

A mild pea flavor is displayed in this soup along with the hint of fresh dill, which is a great starter to any spring dinner.

5 cups pea pods

2 cups chicken stock
   (see page 192 for recipe)

2 cups water

1 cup onion, chopped

2 tablespoons olive oil

¼ cup fresh dill

1 cup heavy cream

Salt and pepper, to taste

In a large pot, heat oil over medium heat. Add onion and cook until softened, 5 to 10 minutes. Add the chicken stock and water and increase heat to bring to a boil. Add pea pods and cook until tender. Add the fresh herbs and salt and pepper to taste.

Remove from heat and allow mixture to cool slightly. Pour half of the mixture into a blender and blend until soup is smooth. Repeat with the excess mixture. Return soup mixture to large pot and add heavy cream. Bring mixture back up to temperature.

Garnish with fresh herbs and serve.

Roasted Spring Veggies

SERVES 8

Any combination of fresh vegetables can be used in this recipe, but cooking time may vary depending on what you choose. While fennel and carrots are not available from the garden in early spring, I've included them here because I find that they make for a classic springtime flavor combo. They also pair beautifully with ham or lamb, making them a frequent feature in Easter meals.

1 fennel bulb

6 carrots

Olive oil

Salt and pepper, to taste

Preheat oven to 400°F. Wash fennel bulb and remove fronds. Slice fennel into ½-inch slices and place on baking sheet.

Wash and peel carrots. Slice in half and then into quarters, and place on the baking sheet with fennel. Evenly spread out vegetables and drizzle with olive oil. Season with salt and pepper.

Bake vegetables 25 to 30 minutes, until tender and lightly browned.

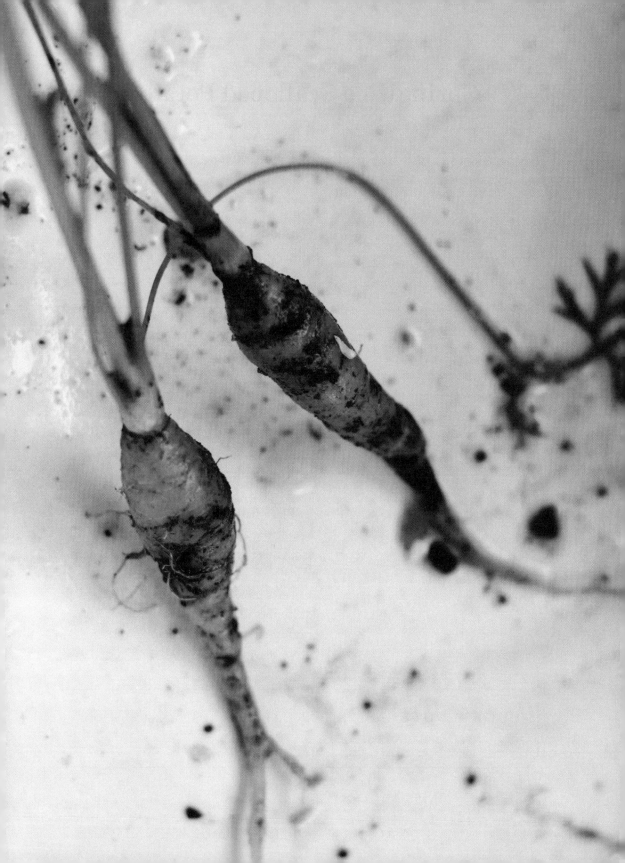

Springtime Scalloped Potatoes

SERVES 8

This decadent side dish is "ramped" up with all the green that comes from the spring warmth in upstate New York; ramps and nettles. The nettles can be omitted.

RAMP PESTO

Ramps, cleaned

Olive oil

Grated Parmesan cheese

Salt and pepper

1 small onion, chopped

2 tablespoons butter

1 cup stinging nettles

½ teaspoon salt

Pepper, to taste

2 tablespoons flour

1¼ cups milk

½ cup prepared ramp pesto

3 cups potatoes, thinly sliced

To make pesto, roughly chop cleaned ramps and place in a blender. Add a generous amount of olive oil, starting at about a half cup per every 10 ramps. Pulse to combine. Add more olive oil if mixture seems too dry. Mixture should resemble almost a fine paste. Add Parmesan, and salt and pepper to taste. Set aside.

Cook onion in butter until tender. Stir in flour, salt, and pepper. Add milk all at once. Cook and stir until thickened and bubbly. Add nettle and stir to coat and combine. Remove from heat. Stir in prepared ramp pesto.

Place half of the sliced potatoes in the bottom of a greased 1-quart casserole dish. Cover with half of the sauce. Repeat in layers.

Bake covered for 35 minutes. Bake an additional 30 minutes uncovered, or until potatoes are tender. Let stand 5 minutes before serving.

COOK'S NOTE: Pesto can be stored in the freezer for up to one year in a freezer-safe container.

Strawberry Shortcake

SERVES 12

Instead of a traditional shortcake, a buttery pound cake is used for this classic seasonal dessert. Chocolate or lemon can also be used to add a flavorful twist.

POUND CAKE

1¾ cups flour

½ teaspoon salt

1 cup butter, softened

1½ cups sugar

3 eggs

1¼ teaspoons vanilla extract

¼ cup whole milk

STRAWBERRIES

1 quart strawberries

½ cup sugar

Lemon zest

WHIPPED CREAM

1 pint heavy cream

¼ cup sugar

1 teaspoon vanilla extract

Heat oven to 350°F. Butter and flour a metal loaf pan. Whisk flour and salt in medium bowl. With an electric mixer, beat butter until fluffy. Gradually beat in sugar until blended. Beat in eggs one at a time, scraping down the sides of bowl. Beat in vanilla. Beat in half of the flour mixture, then milk, then remaining flour.

Spread batter evenly in the prepared pan and bake cake until golden, and a tester inserted into the center comes out clean—about 1 hour and 15 minutes. Cool cake in pan for 10 minutes. Cut around sides of pan to loosen and turn cake onto rack. Turn right side up and allow to cool completely.

Wash and dry strawberries. Slice to desired thickness and place in a medium bowl. Add sugar and lemon zest and stir to coat. Let stand for 1 hour before serving to allow strawberries and sugar to macerate.

Just before serving, combine all the ingredients for whipped cream in a mixing bowl and whip with an electric mixer until stiff peaks form.

Slice pound cake and serve with strawberries and whipped cream.

The Westkill

MAKES 1

This refreshing cocktail features one of my favorite drink mixers—shrub, which dates back to colonial America. The tartness of the vinegar and rhubarb is balanced by the strawberries and sugar.

STRAWBERRY RHUBARB SHRUB

1 cup rhubarb, chopped

1 cup strawberries, sliced

1 cup cider vinegar

2 cups sugar

COCKTAIL

1 ounce gin

1 ounce strawberry rhubarb shrub

½ ounce elderflower liqueur

Club soda

Ice

To make shrub, combine rhubarb, strawberries, sugar, and vinegar in a medium saucepan. Cook over medium heat until mixture begins to boil, stirring frequently. Remove from heat and let stand for 1 hour.

Press mixture through a fine-mesh sieve into a bowl and discard solids. Pour syrup into a large mason jar, cover, and chill for 1 hour before using.

To make the drink, combine 3 to 4 ice cubes, gin, shrub, and elderflower liqueur in a cocktail shaker, and shake for 30 seconds. Pour into glass and top with club soda.

COOK'S NOTE: Shrub can be stored in the fridge for one week.

Summer

Cacio e Pepe with Greens

SERVES 2

Pasta is my go-to dinner almost anytime I cook for just myself. Adding the baby greens to this dish creates a whole new dimension, both texture and flavor-wise. Be sure to use freshly ground black pepper to achieve the best flavor.

6 ounces thin spaghetti

4 tablespoons butter

1 teaspoon freshly cracked
    black pepper

1 cup finely grated
    Parmesan cheese

¾ cup reserved pasta water

1 cup baby spinach

1 cup arugula

Salt and pepper, to taste

Bring water to a boil in a 5-quart pot. Season with salt. Add pasta and cook, stirring occasionally, until about 2 minutes before al dente. Drain, reserving ¾ cup pasta cooking water.

Melt 3 tablespoons butter in the same pot the pasta was cooked in, over medium heat. Add pepper and cook, swirling pan, until toasted, about 1 minute.

Add ½ cup reserved pasta water to pot and bring to a simmer. Add pasta and remaining butter. Reduce heat to low and add cheese, stirring and tossing with tongs until melted. Add greens and continue to toss until combined and greens are some-what wilted. Add more pasta water if sauce seems dry. Transfer pasta to warm bowls and serve.

Swiss Chard Gratin

SERVES 8

This dish is a great change of pace from simply steamed or sautéed Swiss chard. Any cheese can be used in this dish such as smoked gouda or goat cheese.

2 pounds Swiss chard, including half of stems

4 tablespoons butter

1 onion, finely chopped

Salt and pepper, to taste

1 cup breadcrumbs

1 clove garlic, minced

3 tablespoons chopped parsley

1 tablespoon flour

1 cup milk

1 cup sharp cheddar cheese (shredded)

Heat oven to 400°F.

Wash and dry chard. Separate leaves and stems. Coarsely chop leaves and dice stems into small pieces.

Melt 1 tablespoon butter in a large skillet over medium heat. Add onion and stems and cook, stirring occasionally until onion begins to brown, about 20 minutes. Add leaves, season with 1 teaspoon salt, and cook until wilted and tender, about 10 minutes.

Meanwhile, lightly grease a 2-quart baking dish. Melt remaining 2 tablespoons butter in a small skillet and add breadcrumbs, minced garlic, and parsley. Cook, stirring for 1 minute, then transfer to a small bowl and return skillet to the heat.

Melt the remaining 1 tablespoon of butter, stir in flour, and whisk in the milk. Simmer for 5 minutes and season with ½ teaspoon salt. Add to the chard mixture. Add cheese and season with salt and pepper to taste.

Pour mixture into prepared dish and cover with breadcrumb mixture. Bake until heated through and golden on top, about 25 minutes. Let stand before serving.

Milkweed Blossom Fritters

SERVES 4-6

Milkweed blossoms should be harvested when they are just about to flower and are slightly purple in hue, but are not in bloom.

BEER BATTER

1 (12-ounce) can light beer

1½ cups flour

Oil for frying

3 cups milkweed blossoms

Old Bay seasoning

Ranch dressing

Make the batter and heat 1 inch of oil in a medium skillet. When oil is hot enough, dip blossoms in batter to fully coat, allowing excess to drip off, and place them in skillet.

Fry blossoms in several batches so that the skillet is not crowded. When one side of fritter is golden, flip to brown the other side. Remove and place on paper towel-lined plate and sprinkle with Old Bay.

Serve immediately with ranch dressing as a dipping sauce.

HORTON HILL FARM

JEFFERSON, NY

FOOD. GOOD FOOD. Really good food! Delicious food! Bill and Carol Parker believe that life should revolve around food. There is nothing better than sharing delicious food with family and friends—in fact, the best culinary experiences are when family and friends are gathered around the table, being provided with the healthiest and best food from local sources. Enjoying a meal with meats, vegetables and beverages grown on their farm or grown by their local neighbors is very important to them. They believe that knowing where and how their food is grown inspires them to do what they do.

On Horton Hill Farm, in addition to the huge vegetable garden, fruit trees, and bushes, chickens are raised (for eggs and meat), alongside pigs, turkeys and honeybees. All of the animals are raised on green pastures and fed grain from the local feed mill. The Parkers believe that the combination of good genetics, green grass and sunshine creates the healthiest and most delicious meats that you can find.

Horton Hill Farm had its beginning after the birth of Bill and Carol's daughter, Kelly. They felt it was important for her to eat antibiotic-free and healthy foods. The Parkers bought a few meat chicks and a couple of piglets, but soon enough others began asking for the locally sourced meats. Their pasture-raised farm was born.

They made a farm and family decision to raise only heritage breed pigs, turkeys and laying chickens. Heritage livestock are the type of animals that would have been raised one hundred years ago: these animals are slower growing, but have superior flavor. These animals take a longer amount of time to reach processing weight, and in a world where time is money this is unpopular with larger farms, but the Parkers know that this extra time is an acceptable trade-off for better quality and flavor.

Horton Hill Farm strives to produce a high-quality product. They realize that most locally grown foods have a higher cost than the store-bought foods, but the taste, flavor, and texture of a healthier and drug-free product for their family to eat is worth the price.

As a consumer, you should know who your farmer is. Ask about their farm practices; visit the farm and look at their animals. Only then will you truly know that you are putting the best possible meats on your table for your family and friends to enjoy.

Honey Brined Pork Chops

SERVES 4

Brining meats ensures that you will have delicious meats every time. The water in the brine adds more moisture to your meat, resulting in a juicier and more flavorful meal, while the salt dissolves proteins, resulting in a more tender piece of meat.

BRINE

3 cups water

¼ cup Kosher salt

¼ cup raw honey

4 pasture raised pork chops

Raw honey

To make the brine, combine water, salt and honey in a medium saucepan. Heat mixture until honey and salt dissolves. Cool.

Add pork chops to brine. Be sure that are chops are covered with the brine. Brine for 4 to 8 hours.

Bring pork chops to room temperature and pat them dry. Heat your grill, creating a hot side and a less hot side. Sear chops for 2 minutes per side on the hot side of the grill, then move your chops to the less hot side of the grill to continue slow cooking. Grill, turning the chops until their internal temperature reaches 145°F.

Remove chops from grill and smear with raw honey. Let rest, covered with foil for 5 to 10 minutes. Enjoy with local vegetables and your favorite mead.

Stuffed Squash Blossoms

SERVES 5

The ratio of meat to rice in this recipe can be adjusted based on personal preference. The cheese variety is also left open-ended, making this dish endlessly customizable.

Oil for frying

10 squash blossoms

1 cup cooked rice

¼–½ cup shredded cooked chicken or cooked crumbled sausage

¼ cup shredded cheese

¼ cup chopped fresh herbs

Salt and pepper, to taste

Ranch dressing

BATTER

1 cup flour

1 cup water

Rinse blossoms and remove stamen from the center.

Prepare batter by combining flour and water and whisking until smooth. Combine rice, chicken or sausage, cheese, herbs, and salt and pepper to taste. Stuff each blossom with 1 tablespoon of filling, but be careful not to over-stuff.

Meanwhile, heat 1 inch of oil in a skillet. Coat blossoms with batter and place in hot oil. When one side of the blossom is golden brown, flip to brown the other side. Fry blossoms in batches so the pan is not crowded. Transfer cooked blossoms onto paper towel-lined plate. Serve with ranch dressing for dipping.

Zucchini Fritters

SERVES 4

This dish is a great way to utilize the surplus of zucchini that always seems to come about in mid-summer. At my house, we typically serve these as appetizers to a summer meal out on the patio or as a side to grilled marinated venison steaks, but feel free to pair them with any dish that needs a savory side.

SOY DIPPING SAUCE

3 tablespoons rice vinegar

1 tablespoon soy sauce

1 teaspoon honey

½ teaspoon red pepper flakes

FRITTERS

1½ pounds zucchini, grated

½ teaspoon salt

1 large egg

¼ cup flour

3 tablespoons fresh chives, chopped

1 tablespoon cornstarch

Black pepper, to taste

⅓ cup vegetable oil

Mix all ingredients for dipping sauce in a bowl and set aside.

Place zucchini in a colander placed in the sink and toss with salt. Squeeze zucchini dry in clean kitchen towel. Place zucchini in a large bowl and mix in egg, flour, chives, and cornstarch until combined. Season with salt and pepper.

Heat oil in a large skillet over medium heat. Drop ¼ cup zucchini mixture into pan and flatten slightly. Cook fritters until golden and crisp, about 3 minutes on each side. Work in batches until batter is gone. Place on a plate and season with salt. Serve with soy dipping sauce.

Zucchini Swiss Chard Soup

SERVES 8

While soup may not sound appealing during the summer months, this one is sure to please with its lightness, as well as the amount of vegetables packed into it.

1 pound zucchini

½ pound Swiss chard
   leaves

½ cup onion, chopped

2 tablespoons olive oil

1 cup cooked white rice

5-6 cups chicken stock
   (see page 192 for recipe)

Salt and pepper, to taste

Grated Parmesan cheese,
   to taste

Wash, trim, and grate zucchini. Wash chard leaves, discarding any tough ribs, and shred. Heat oil in a large stock pot. Cook onions over medium heat, stirring occasionally, 4 to 5 minutes.

Add the grated zucchini and shredded chard and cook for 5 minutes. Stir in rice and stock. Add salt and pepper to taste. Bring soup to boil and allow to simmer for 30 minutes. Add grated Parmesan to taste and serve.

Dilly Beans

YIELDS 4 PINTS (2 QUARTS)

Pickling is a great way to preserve excess vegetables for enjoyment later on in the year. As an added plus, you don't need many supplies to pickle at home: just some jars, lids (always use new) and bands, a large pot, and the ingredients for the recipe, typically involving pickling salt, spices and vinegar. Try using these spicy beans in your next Bloody Mary!

2 pounds green or yellow beans

¼ cup canning salt

2½ cups vinegar

2½ cups water

1 teaspoon cayenne pepper

4 cloves garlic

4 heads dill

Trim ends off beans. Combine salt, vinegar, and water in a large saucepan and bring to a boil. Pack beans lengthwise into hot jars, leaving a ¼-inch headspace. Add ¼ teaspoon cayenne pepper, 1 clove garlic, and 1 head dill to each pint jar. If using quart jars, add ½ teaspoon cayenne pepper, 2 cloves garlic, and 2 heads dill to each jar.

Ladle hot liquid over beans, leaving a ¼-inch headspace. Remove air bubbles. Adjust two-piece caps. Process pints and quarts for 10 minutes in a boiling water canner.

Green Beans with Garlic

SERVES 4

We normally grow a large quantity of bush and pole beans in the garden, so come July we tend to have a surplus. Most of these will end up frozen, but the remainder is saved for a spicy dinner side, like these!

1 pound fresh green beans

4 large garlic cloves

Olive oil

Salt and pepper, to taste

Wash beans and remove ends. Steam beans until bright green and still crisp.

Meanwhile, heat a good amount of olive oil in a large sauté pan. Crush garlic cloves and add to hot oil. Cook until slightly browned. Add steamed green beans and toss to coat with garlic and oil. Season with salt and pepper to taste.

COOK'S NOTE: Briefly steaming the beans allows for a brighter green color and preserves their crispiness, so they seem untouched from the garden to plate.

Cucumber Salad

SERVES 4

It seems like everyone has their own special recipe for cucumber salad, and after a summer of cookouts and barbecues, all those mayo-based salads can start to feel a bit redundant and heavy. That's where this dish shines: the combination of rice wine vinegar and fresh dill gives it a very refreshing quality that makes for a perfect summer side that goes with practically anything. Try bringing it to your next summer gathering, or serve it at home alongside grilled chicken or pork.

2 large cucumbers

½ red onion

½ cup rice wine vinegar

2 tablespoons fresh dill, minced

1 teaspoon salt

Slice cucumbers and onion as thin as possible, either with mandolin or by hand. Place in a medium bowl and add dill and vinegar. Mix well and cover.

Refrigerate for at least 20 minutes before serving.

CRYSTAL VALLEY FARM

HALCOTT CENTER, NY

CRYSTAL VALLEY FARM was born out of the long-time dreams of Chris and Judy DiBenedetto. Shortly after getting married, the couple lived at Innisfail Farm, a well-known Milking Shorthorn dairy in Northern California where Judy had worked for several years. Desiring their own farm but recognizing the prohibitive cost of starting a dairy in California, Chris and Judy set their sights eastward to the Catskill Mountains, where Chris had grown up on his family's farm just outside of Fleischmanns. The opportunity to rent a farm in the Denver Valley became available, and in September 1989 the couple and their eight-month-old daughter Elena headed east with a pick-up truck and a U-Haul trailer.

The next few years were exciting times of growth. In 1991, the family welcomed their son Greg into the world, and their dairy herd grew and improved as Chris and Judy gained experience in managing their own farm. To make room for increasing cattle numbers, the herd was moved later that year to a larger farm near the original barn.

Throughout this time, one particular practice became a cornerstone for Crystal Valley Farm: management intensive grazing. Since the small land bases on the rented farms limited the amount of grazing possible, the family wanted to purchase a farm that would offer ample opportunity to set up a complete grazing system. They didn't have to travel far: just one valley over in Halcott Center. When the family's rental farm was sold in 1993, the DiBenedettos and their cattle loaded up and headed to the town of Halcott and settled into what would become their long-term home.

Today, Crystal Valley Farm pastures are home to a colorful herd of about seventy Holstein, Milking Shorthorn, and crossbred milk cows. Calves and some heifers are raised on the farm, while other heifers are boarded out on local farms at various times of the year.

The farm expanded in 2012 by bottling a small portion of its output as pasteurized cream line milk through a neighboring creamery, which began selling them at local outlets. In 2013, the pasteurizing and bottling equipment was relocated

to a small creamery built on the farm where some of the farm's milk is now processed in small batches to supply local customers and businesses with a fresh, healthy, flavorful product. Recently, Crystal Valley has started offering Maple Milk, which uses syrup from local maple producers. Plans are in motion to craft other naturally flavored milks as well.

Over the years and through all the changes, the one constant has been the help and support Crystal Valley Farm has enjoyed from family and friends. Greg and Elena are vital parts of the operation today and both plan to continue their involvement in the family business. Currently, Greg manages the machinery, feeding, cropping, and building parts of the farm, while Elena handles much of the evening milking, record keeping, and other jobs. Truly, their hard work and dedication to this labor of love has helped make dreams come true at Crystal Valley Farm.

Peach & Blackberry Bread Pudding

SERVES 12

Fresh summertime fruit and rich and creamy Crystal Valley Cream Line milk come together to create a decadent dessert. Grilling the sliced peaches covered in sugar and cinnamon creates a robust caramel flavor that adds to the flavor of the pudding.

1 loaf Italian or French bread, cut into cubes (about 8 cups)

3½ cups Cream Line milk

4 peaches, peeled and sliced

1¼ cup sugar

1½ teaspoons cinnamon

2 tablespoons butter

1 cup fresh blackberries

6 eggs

½ teaspoon nutmeg

1 teaspoon vanilla

Whipped cream

Place cubed bread on a sheet tray and let sit out for about an hour. Place bread in a large bowl and pour 3 cups of milk over it, and let sit for 30 minutes, stirring a few times.

Meanwhile, place sliced peaches in a small bowl with ¼ cup sugar and ½ teaspoon cinnamon and toss. Heat grill pan to medium and coat with butter. When hot, place slices on pan, spread apart and cook. Flip peach slices after 2 to 3 minutes when grill marks are clear. Pour any cinnamon sugar liquid over peaches to create a caramelization. Remove peaches and place back in bowl. Add 2 tablespoons of butter and blackberries to the peaches and stir.

Preheat oven to 375°F. Coat a 5 x 9-inch baking dish with butter. In a bowl, whisk eggs, ½ cup milk, 1 cup sugar, 1 teaspoon cinnamon, ½ teaspoon nutmeg and vanilla, until combined. Add egg mixture to bread mixture and stir until combined. Fold in peach mixture. Place the mixture in prepared pan and bake for 45 to 55 minutes until golden brown and a toothpick inserted in the middle comes out clean. Serve warm with whipped cream.

Raspberry Ice Cream Sandwiches

MAKES 12

An ice cream machine is required for this recipe, but investing in one is definitely worth it. Any summer berry can be used in the ice cream, or just classic vanilla.

ICE CREAM

1 cup fresh raspberries

¼ cup sugar, plus ¾ cup

¼ cup water

2 cups chilled heavy cream

1 cup chilled whole milk

1 teaspoon vanilla extract

SHORTBREAD COOKIES

2 cups powdered sugar

2 cups butter, softened

2 egg yolks

4 cups flour

1 cup cornstarch

Cook raspberries, sugar, and water over medium heat in a medium saucepan until raspberries are cooked down. Put raspberry puree through a mesh sieve to remove seeds and set aside.

Place all ice cream ingredients in a medium mixing bowl and combine until well blended. Pour mixture into a frozen ice cream machine bowl and turn the machine on. Mix until mixture is thickened, about 20 to 25 minutes. Place in freezer until firm, about 2 hours.

Meanwhile, combine powdered sugar and butter in a mixing bowl, and beat until fluffy. Add egg yolks and blend well. Add flour and cornstarch and mix well. Divide dough in half, form into a ball and refrigerate until firm.

The Catskills Farm to Table Cookbook

Preheat oven to 350°F. Roll dough to ¼-inch thickness and cut into 2½ x 2½-inch squares. Place on an ungreased baking sheet and bake for 8 to 13 minutes or until lightly browned and set. Prick the tops of the cookies with a fork and remove from baking sheet. Cool completely.

To assemble sandwiches, scoop desired amount of ice cream onto a cookie and top with second cookie. Serve immediately.

Red Currant Mini Cakes

SERVES 4

These little cakes can be eaten at breakfast or be served as a dessert with fresh whipped cream. The red currants can be substituted with any fresh berry like strawberries, blueberries, or blackberries.

½ cup plain whole milk yogurt

1 cup sugar

3 large eggs

½ cup vegetable oil

1½ cups flour

2 teaspoons baking powder

¼ teaspoons salt

1 tablespoons lemon zest

1 cup fresh red currants

Preheat oven to 350°F.

Lightly grease and flour the cups of a mini-loaf pan. In a large bowl, whisk together yogurt, sugar, eggs and oil until smooth and well blended. Add flour, baking powder, salt and lemon zest, and stir until the batter is smooth and silky. Pour into the prepared mini-loaf tin, dividing evenly between the cups. Scatter berries on top of the batter, using around 2 tablespoons per loaf.

Bake for 25 to 30 minutes, or until the edges are pale gold and a toothpick comes out clean when inserted into the center of one loaf. Let cool on a rack for 20 minutes in the pan, then turn out and let cool completely before serving.

Blueberry Tart with Thyme Pastry

SERVES 8

When the same old, same old blueberry tart gets to be too boring and humdrum, I find adding some fresh thyme to the pastry makes all the difference. With its subtle earthy flavor—which pairs so nicely with the tart and sweet blueberries, available in abundance during the summer—it completely revitalizes your taste for this classic treat.

CRUST

Pastry for one-crust pie
  (see page 36 for recipe)

4 fresh thyme sprigs

FILLING

4 cups fresh blueberries

¾ cup sugar

¼ cup flour

¼ teaspoon cinnamon

2 teaspoons lemon juice

Prepare pastry for one-crust pie, adding thyme leaves to flour mixture. Place and form to a circular or rectangular tart pan.

Preheat oven to 425°F. In a large bowl, combine filling ingredients and mix. Spoon into pastry-lined pan. Bake for 45 to 55 minutes. Serve with vanilla ice cream or whipped cream.

COOK'S NOTE: Serve this tart with lightly sweetened whipped cream to balance out all of the flavors.

Blueberry Muffins

MAKES 12

This versatile muffin recipe can be made at any time of year with fresh or frozen fruit, and is a perfect way to highlight whatever fruit is in season.

MUFFINS

1¾ cups flour

⅓ cup sugar

2 teaspoons baking powder

¼ teaspoon salt

1 egg, beaten

¾ cup milk

¼ cup vegetable oil

¾ cup fresh blueberries

1 teaspoon lemon zest

TOPPING

½ cup rolled oats

½ cup butter, melted

¼ cup brown sugar

½ teaspoon cinnamon

Preheat oven to 400°F. Lightly grease muffin tin or line with baking cups. In a medium mixing bowl, combine flour, sugar, baking powder and ¼ teaspoon salt, and make a well in the center. Combine egg, milk, and oil in a separate bowl. Add all to flour mixture. Stir until just moistened. Fold in blueberries and lemon zest.

Fill muffin cups until almost full. Spoon topping mixture over batter. Bake until golden, about 20 minutes. Remove from pan and serve warm.

Pickled Red Onions

YIELDS 6 HALF-PINTS

Here you have it: the essential condiment for summer gatherings. These pickled onions go great on pretty much everything: hot dogs, burgers, tacos, avocado toast... My personal favorite is on fresh venison bratwurst patties (as shown), but Italian sausage works well, too. Great taste and a vibrant pop of color—you really can't go wrong!

3 pounds red onions

4 cups red wine vinegar

1 clove garlic

Peel onions and slice ¼-inch thick, separating the slices into rings. Bring vinegar and garlic to a boil, before reducing heat and let simmer for 5 minutes. Add onion rings to vinegar and simmer, covered, for 5 minutes.

Discard garlic. Pack hot onions into hot jars, leaving ¼-inch headspace. Remove air bubbles. Adjust two-piece caps. Process for 10 minutes in a boiling water canner.

Corn Chowder

SERVES 8

This vibrant soup has a Southwestern flavor that highlights both the sweetness of corn but also the complexity of the sausage.

2 tablespoons olive oil

1 cup onion, chopped

½ cup celery, diced

1 cup green pepper, chopped

2 cloves garlic, minced

½ teaspoon cayenne pepper

1 pound smoked andouille sausage, cooked and crumbled

3 cups corn kernels

Bay leaf

2 teaspoons dried thyme

6 cups chicken stock (see page 192 for recipe)

3 potatoes, cubed

1 cup heavy cream

Salt and pepper, to taste

Heat olive oil in a large pot over medium-high heat. Cook onion, celery, green bell pepper, until softened, about 5 minutes. Stir garlic, cayenne pepper, and crumbled andouille sausage into the onion mixture; continue to cook and stir until the sausage is hot, 1 to 2 minutes more.

Fold corn kernels and bay leaves into the sausage mixture; season with thyme. Allow the mixture to simmer until the corn is warmed, about 1 minute. Add chicken stock and bring mixture to a boil, reduce heat to medium-low, and cook at a simmer, stirring occasionally, about 30 minutes.

Stir potatoes and heavy cream into the pot. Cover and continue cooking at a simmer until the potatoes are tender, about 20 minutes. Season with salt and black pepper.

Squash Noodles

SERVES 4

Zucchini and yellow squash are among the most abundant of the veggies harvested during the summer months, and with a constant surplus comes the constant struggle to find new ways to cook with them. Summer squash works well as noodles thanks to its mild flavor, and can be served cold as a salad or hot as a side dish.

2 medium zucchini

2 medium yellow squash

1 cup cherry tomatoes, halved

Olive oil

PESTO

1 cup fresh basil leaves

5 cloves garlic

½ cup olive oil

¼ cup Parmesan cheese

Salt and pepper, to taste

To make noodles, put squash through a spiralizer. Heat olive oil in a large sauté pan and add noodles.

Meanwhile, place basil, garlic, olive oil, and Parmesan cheese in a food processor and blend until combined and smooth. Add salt and pepper to taste.

Add prepared pesto to noodles and toss to coat. Add cherry tomatoes and cook until heated. Season with additional salt and pepper if needed.

Peach Pie

SERVES 12

If there was a fruit to perfectly encapsulate summer in the Catskills, it would be the peach. Fresh peaches are available at farm stands the region over, usually as soon as they come in season (though, if you are really lucky, you'll have a neighbor down the road with a peach tree of their own, willing to share!) The vibrant flavor of ripe peaches is truly given room to shine in this classic pie.

CRUST

Pastry for one-crust pie
   (see page 36 for recipe)

FILLING

4 cups sliced peeled
   peaches

½ cup sugar

¼ cup flour

½ teaspoon cinnamon

2 tablespoons butter

TOPPING

Milk

Sugar

Cinnamon

Prepare pastry by doubling recipe for one-crust pie. Place half of the pastry into a 9-inch pie plate.

Preheat oven to 375°F. In a large bowl, combine filling ingredients and toss gently. Spoon into pastry-lined pie plate. Dot filling with butter and top with remaining pastry. Fold and crimp edges of pastry together and cut slits into top. Brush pastry with milk and sprinkle with sugar and cinnamon. Bake for 45 to 55 minutes until top is golden brown. Serve with vanilla ice cream or whipped cream.

COOK'S NOTE: If fresh peaches are not available or are out of season, feel free to substitute frozen peaches, remembering to drain off any excess liquid.

Tomato Sandwich

MAKES 1 SANDWICH

When tomato season rolls around, I can hardly wait to make my first tomato sandwich. Usually I'll make one for breakfast...and then one for lunch...and maybe one as a snack before dinner? Truth be told, I don't really consider it to be summer until tomato juice is dripping down my hands as I savor every ounce of a ripe tomato. You can easily top this sandwich with baby arugula and/or thinly sliced red onion for an elevated version, or else stick with the classic of mayo, olive oil, red pepper flakes, curry powder, salt and pepper.

2 slices peasant bread

1 clove garlic

1–2 tomatoes, sliced

Olive oil

Flaked sea salt

Mayonnaise

Red pepper flakes

Pepper

Toast the bread. Take each slice and rub one side with the garlic clove. Spread desired amount of mayonnaise onto each slice of toast. Place sliced tomato onto one slice of toast and drizzle with olive oil. Sprinkle tomatoes with salt, pepper, and pepper flakes. Top with remaining slice of toast and cut in half. Serve immediately.

Pasta with Blistered Tomatoes

SERVES 4

An abundance of cherry tomatoes is inevitable, and this is a great and simple dish to utilize them. The tomatoes can also be used by themselves in other dishes, like a topping for cod.

1 pound dry pasta

Olive oil

2 cups cherry tomatoes

2 tablespoons fresh
   oregano

Salt and pepper, to taste

Parmesan cheese, to taste

Quarter cherry tomatoes and place on a baking sheet. Drizzle with olive oil and season with salt and pepper. Broil tomatoes on high until they begin to shrivel. Remove and toss with fresh oregano.

Meanwhile, cook pasta in boiling, salted water, until al dente. Drain and return to pot. Add tomatoes and additional olive oil. Season with salt and pepper and serve with grated Parmesan cheese.

Caprese Bruschetta

SERVING VARIES

While this recipe involves virtually no cooking (save for a quick toasting of the bread), it is this simplicity that makes it a perfect summer dish. Simple summery ingredients come together quickly and effortlessly, presenting themselves beautifully on a platter to create the ideal dish to serve at impromptu summer get-togethers.

French baguette

Olive oil

Garlic cloves

Fresh mozzarella

Tomatoes

Basil leaves

Balsamic vinegar

Slice baguette into ½-inch slices. Arrange on a baking sheet and brush each slice with olive oil. Broil on high until lightly browned. Rub garlic clove on each slice and arrange slices on a serving tray. Slice mozzarella and tomato and arrange on the same serving tray. Place fresh basil leaves on tray. Have balsamic vinegar available for drizzling.

COOK'S NOTE: There are no proper amounts or measurements for this recipe; prepare as much or as little as your hungry guests will eat!

Tomato Salad

SERVES 6

The freshness of summer tomato, the crisp, crunchiness of cucumber, combined with aromatic basil and spicy red onion? This is a summer salad without equal, one that pairs the best of your garden or fresh market ingredients.

3 cups cherry tomatoes, quartered

1 cucumber, peeled

1 red onion

¼ cup fresh basil

¼ cup olive oil

¼ cup balsamic vinegar

Salt and pepper, to taste

Place quartered cherry tomatoes in a medium serving bowl. Quarter cucumber and add to bowl. Thinly slice red onion and add to tomato and cucumber mixture. Coarsely chop basil leaves and add.

Combine olive oil and vinegar in a small bowl and mix until combined; add to salad and toss to coat. Season with salt and pepper to taste. Chill salad if not serving immediately.

COOK'S NOTE: Cubed mozzarella can be added to this salad for an added kick. You can also substitute avocado for the cucumbers.

BBQ Chicken

SERVES 4

This is an adaptation of the Cornell marinade, which was developed by a professor at Cornell University who wanted to create an opportunity for local farmers to sell more chicken. It can be stored, covered in the fridge for a few weeks.

4 chicken halves

MARINADE

1 cup cooking oil

1 pint cider vinegar

3 tablespoons salt

1 tablespoon Old Bay seasoning

½ teaspoon dried sage

½ teaspoon pepper

1 egg

Beat egg, then add oil and beat to combine. Add other ingredients and stir.

Place the chicken halves over the fire after the flame is gone. Turn the halves every 5 to 10 minutes, depending on the heat from the fire. Use turners or a long-handled fork. The chicken should be basted with a brush at each turning. The basting should be light at first and heavy near the end of the cooking period.

Test the chicken to see whether it is done by pulling the wing away from the body and using a meat thermometer. If the meat in this area splits easily and the meat thermometer reads at least 165°F in the breast and thigh, the chicken is done.

Grilled Corn on the Cob

MAKES 8

Grilling corn on the cob (instead of just boiling it) adds a whole new depth of flavor, but we all know corn on the cob really isn't complete without butter. This is my personal recipe for herb butter, but you can add any fresh herbs you have on hand and make this one your own. I especially like the combo of fresh tarragon or dill with corn.

8 ears corn

Salt

Herb butter (see below)

HERB BUTTER

2 sticks butter, softened

¼ cup chopped fresh herbs (basil, chives or tarragon)

1 teaspoon salt

Pepper, to taste

To make herb butter, combine all ingredients in a food processor and process until smooth.

Heat the grill to medium. Pull the outer husks down the ear to the base of the corn. Remove silk from each ear of corn by hand. Fold husks back into place, and place the ears of corn in a large bowl of cold water with 1 tablespoon of salt for 10 minutes.

Remove corn from water and shake off the excess. Place the corn on the grill, close the cover and grill for 15 to 20 minutes, turning every 5 minutes, or until kernels are tender when pierced with a knife.

Remove the husks and serve with prepared herb butter. Spread over the corn while hot.

COOK'S NOTE: If you find you've made too much herb butter, the excess can be frozen for later use.

Peach Crisp

SERVES 6

A crisp is a great way to use excess fruit and is also perfect for get-togethers because it is not fussy to make or to serve.

FILLING

6 cups sliced peaches

1 teaspoon cinnamon

1 tablespoon water

1 teaspoon lemon juice

TOPPING

1 cup rolled oats

¾ cup flour

¾ cup brown sugar

½ cup butter, softened

Preheat oven to 375°F. Place peaches in an 8-inch square baking dish. Sprinkle with cinnamon, water, and lemon juice.

In a large bowl, combine all topping ingredients, and mix until crumbly. Sprinkle crumb topping evenly over peaches. Bake until fruit is tender and topping is golden brown, 25 to 35 minutes. Serve warm with vanilla ice cream or whipped cream.

Blackberry Gin & Tonic

MAKES 1

Gin and tonics are a popular summer drink, and it just so happens that blackberries are in season during late summer in the Catskills. I myself have a large patch of wild blackberries growing in the pasture behind my house where I spend hours carefully harvesting them. While I usually make a jam with them bulk of my crop, the excess is perfect for making drinks.

BLACKBERRY SIMPLE SYRUP

1 cup blackberries

1 cup sugar

½ cup water

½ ounce fresh lime juice

1 ounce blackberry simple syrup

1½ ounces gin

Tonic water

Ice

Lime wedge

Blackberries

To make simple syrup, combine blackberries, sugar and water in a medium saucepan over medium-high heat. Bring mixture to a boil and cook until berries begin to break down, about 5 to 7 minutes. Remove from heat and strain through a fine mesh strainer. Cool completely before using.

Fill cocktail shaker with ice and add simple syrup, lime juice and gin. Shake.

Fill a glass with ice. Strain drink into glass. Top with tonic water and stir. Garnish with blackberries and lime wedge.

COOK'S NOTE: Leftover simple syrup can be stored in a sealed glass jar and kept in the fridge for up to two weeks.

The Catskills Farm to Table Cookbook

Fall

Fried Green Tomatoes

SERVES 4

From now on, there should be no reason to abandon unripe tomatoes in the garden before a frost, because this recipe is sure to please! The dipping sauce can be made with whatever proportions fit your desired flavor preferences.

Oil for frying

4 green tomatoes

3 eggs, beaten

2 cups breadcrumbs

Salt and pepper, to taste

DIPPING SAUCE

Ranch dressing

Frank's Red Hot sauce

Cumin

Chili powder

Combine desired amount of dipping sauce ingredients in a small bowl and set aside.

Wash tomatoes and cut into ¼ or ½-inch slices. Coat with egg and then breadcrumbs seasoned with salt and pepper. When tomatoes are breaded, place in a large frying pan with heated oil. Cook on one side until browned and flip to cook the other side.

Remove from pan and place on a paper towel-lined plate. Serve immediately with prepared dipping sauce.

Roasted Tomatoes

MAKES 24

These tomatoes are great to store in the freezer for adding to sauces later on. Use the desired amount to match your taste preferences.

6 plum tomatoes

Olive oil

Dried oregano

Minced garlic

Salt and pepper, to taste

Preheat oven to 375°F. Slice tomatoes lengthwise into four slices and arrange in one layer on a baking sheet. Drizzle tomatoes with olive oil and top with oregano, garlic, salt and pepper.

Bake just until tomatoes have begun to shrink in size. Remove from oven and let cool completely. Use tomatoes immediately or place in freezer bags or containers for later use.

THE
BULL
&
GARLAND

Pub & In

THE BULL & GARLAND

HOBART, NY

IN 2014, OLIVER and Melissa Pycroft traded the busy streets of London for a small cabin in the Catskill Mountains. After two decades of traveling—working and living in New York City, Paris, London, Budapest and Seville—the couple were ready to escape the cities for the countryside and begin a new, more rural life together.

They set their sights on the Catskill Mountains of New York. It made sense: Melissa's great-grandfather had built several cabins there, and after a visit with their family to the region earlier that year, they fell in love with it.

When Melissa and Oliver decided to move, there wasn't a "plan," per se. They'd always talked about opening a pub or inn together: Oliver had over a decade experience managing pubs and restaurants in London and Nottingham, and Melissa was an artist who had worked as a project manager in the non-profits sector. Their combined experience and shared passions were perfect for such an endeavor, but first they'd need to find a location. Adding to the matter, the day they moved to the Catskills, the couple found out they were pregnant.

And so, the search for a suitable property needed to be expedited. They landed on a property known as the MacArthur house in the village of Hobart, near the western edge of the Catskills. The building was erected in the 1830s and had been a coaching inn before it became a private residence. As to why they fell in love with it: "The rambling 1830s interior with its quirky rooms and cozy nooks felt like the country pubs we loved to frequent in England," Melissa told us. "We imagined the grounds backing onto the West Branch of the Delaware River as the perfect space for a beer garden."

The couple spent the next year renovating the space. In February 2015, Melissa and Oliver welcomed their daughter Isadora into the world, and in October 2016, the Bull & Garland opened its doors.

The interiors are designed by Melissa, whose artistic background is evident in each room. Each room's attention to detail, plus the use of color, space, and texture, is outstanding. The inn's three rooms sit above the restaurant on the second floor in different shapes and sizes, all beautiful. Stepping into the bar and restaurant transports you to a different world. You no longer feel like you are in Hobart, NY, but in a small town in England.

The English pub-style menu features dishes like Scotch eggs, fish and chips, and sticky toffee pudding. The bar offers both English beers as well as craft brews native to New York State. The weekends offer signature craft cocktails featuring seasonal ingredients and combinations. The menu also changes seasonally. Ingredients from local farms are used in the dishes, including locally grown edible flowers in the cocktails.

Hobart is a little over three hours from NYC, but don't let that deter you. Much of the journey is through long stretches of beautiful road over rolling hills, past barns and rivers. And though the English-style pub and inn is reason enough to visit, the village is near Roxbury and Bovina.

When visiting the Bull & Garland, one feels a strong sense of community. Whether you are sitting at the bar on a Friday or Saturday evening or dining in the dining room, there is always someone you know walking through the door or already seated. Even if you don't know anyone—perhaps you're a visitor staying for the weekend—there is bound to be something held in common with the Bull & Garland's patrons, and a conversation is sure to be struck up over fantastic food and drink in the little village of Hobart.

Chicken Pie

MAKES 4

A rich and flavorful filling of both chicken and ham encased in a buttery and flaky pastry is one of the best meals off the menu at the Bull & Garland. Of course, it pairs wonderfully with a pint and great company.

1 whole chicken

5 large onions

3 large leeks

4 sheets puff pastry

1 (8-ounce) ham steak

1 scant tablespoon dried sage

1 scant tablespoon white pepper

3 bay leaves

3 cloves of garlic

1 tablespoon peppercorns

1 stick butter

½ cup all-purpose flour

1 teaspoon chicken base

½ cup chopped parsley

Start by placing the chicken in a large pot along with 1 large onion (quartered with the skin left on), the green tops of the leaks, peppercorns, bay leaves and a generous pinch of sea salt. Fill pot with water to cover the chicken and bring to a boil. Allow to boil for 10 minutes. Take off the heat and let stand for 25 minutes. Doneness will depend on the size of the chicken. Test with a thermometer.

While the chicken stands, start making your pie cases. Cut the bases from the puff pastry sheets and blind bake them by placing a balled piece of kitchen foil big enough to fill the void in the middle of the individual pie mold. Cook as per the instructions of the pastry brand you are using (usually 15 minutes at around 375°F). Once this initial cook time is up, remove the balled foil and gently push down on the pastry that has puffed into the center of the pie, moving it back toward the walls and cook for a further 2 minutes.

Remove from the oven and allow to rest. Once cool enough to handle, cut the pastry that has risen above the mold with a bread knife and leave the pastry base in the pie mold. These off cuts are tasty morsels of puff

pastry and can prove difficult to avoid snacking on while completing the pies!

Cut the pie lids wide enough so that they overhang the base by ¾-inch all around the circumference (a small plate makes a great template). Then, make eight cuts an inch deep around the edge (think of slicing a pizza but just heading a short way across). These cuts are for the very picturesque and relatively easy to do pleated edges. If you like, however, you can just skip this and use a regular flat lid pressed onto the rim of the base when the time comes. It is essential to place these lids in the refrigerator while you finish preparing the pie mix, otherwise your pastry will not rise properly.

Remove the chicken from the pot and let cool. Strain the stock left in the pot into a smaller pan and place back on the heat and reduce by half (about 1½ pints). This will help concentrate the flavor for the all-important gravy.

While the stock reduces and when the chicken is cool enough to handle, strip the meat from the chicken carcass and shred.

continued on the next page

Once the stock has reduced by half, strain into a separate pan, discarding the onion and aromatics. Melt ½ stick of butter into a saucepan. When the butter is melted, slowly whisk in ½ cup of flour, adding a little a time. Once the flour and butter forms to a smooth paste (a roux), take the stock and add it in, slowly whisking as you go. The aim is to is to get to a

consistency with the gravy that coats the back of a serving spoon with a thick creamy texture. Too loose and your pies will be watery; too thick, and they will be stodgy. Once you are happy with the texture, stir in a teaspoon of chicken base (I like Better than Bullion for its roasted chicken taste), the white pepper, and the ground sage and chopped parsley. Adjust seasoning to taste.

To prepare the base of your pie mix, dice onions into ¼-inch pieces and sweat down in a little oil and butter until they are translucent and slightly caramelized, but not too colored. Chop ham into ¼-inch square pieces and add to the onions. Finally, thoroughly wash and thinly slice leeks and add them to the pan. Sweat them until they are yielding, but don't overcook them; otherwise, you will lose the earthy, sweet and sour taste they bring to the filling. Stir in fresh chopped parsley.

Place the chicken and the leek, onion and ham mix in a bowl and coat them generously with gravy. The aim is not to have the meat and vegetables swimming in the gravy so go steady, taking a sample bite here and there until you like what you taste.

Spoon the pie mix into the blind baked pastry bases. Heap the mix so that it just crests above the top of the pie mold. Next, remove your pre-cut pie lids from the refrigerator. Make a quick egg wash by beating 2 eggs and ½ cup of milk together in a mixing bowl. Using a pastry brush, paint the egg wash around the pastry circumference. Place the lid over the pie mold, maintaining an even overhang on all sides. To pleat the edges, with one hand simply lift one of the pastry tabs to create a small tube and with the other hand, pinch the edge of the adjacent tab to create a kind of hollow ridge. Work in one direction around the edge of the pie, creating a crown-like appearance by pressing the lid down on the base. When this is done, brush the entire lid with the egg wash and place in the oven for another 15 minutes.

Remove from the oven and once cool enough, remove from the pie molds and serve with mashed potatoes or thick fries and the remaining gravy.

Late Season Tomato Soup

SERVES 8

This creamy and flavorful soup can also be made in the summer, but is a great way to find a use for the last of the ripe tomatoes from the garden.

1 tablespoon olive oil

1 onion, diced

2 cloves garlic, minced

2 tablespoons butter

3 tablespoons flour

3 cups chicken stock
(see page 192 for recipe)

6–7 cups tomatoes, roughly
chopped

1 tablespoon balsamic
vinegar

2 tablespoons fresh basil,
chopped

¼ teaspoon celery seed

1 teaspoon paprika

¼ cup milk

Salt and pepper, to taste

Heat olive oil in a large pot over medium heat. Add onion and garlic and cook until soft, about 7 minutes. Add butter and melt. Whisk in flour and mix to coat.

Continue to cook for a minute longer. Whisk in stock. Add tomatoes, vinegar, basil, celery seed, paprika, salt and pepper. Bring contents to a boil and reduce heat and simmer for 10 to 15 minutes or until tomatoes have cooked down.

Remove from heat and stir in milk. Blend soup with an immersion blender until smooth. Season with more salt and pepper if needed.

Beet Greens & Swiss Chard with Garlic

SERVES 4

A mixture of garden greens gives this dish its robust flavor. The addition of fresh tomato and breadcrumbs add another textural element that ties everything together.

TOPPING

1 large tomato, diced

1 tablespoon olive oil

1 garlic clove, minced

1 tablespoon fresh basil, chopped

2 tablespoons olive oil

3 clove garlic, thinly sliced

¼ teaspoon red pepper flakes

GREENS

½ pound beet greens, washed

½ pound Swiss chard, washed

Salt and pepper, to taste

½ cup panko breadcrumbs

1 tablespoon Parmesan cheese

To make the topping, stir together all topping ingredients in a small bowl and set aside.

In a large skillet, heat oil over medium heat. Add the garlic and cook until golden, 1 to 2 minutes. Add the red pepper flakes and stir. Add greens to the skillet and season with salt and pepper to taste. Cover and cook until greens are wilted, 5 minutes. Add breadcrumbs and stir to combine. Cook for 3 minutes more. Serve greens topped with prepared tomato mixture and grated cheese.

Roasted Cauliflower

SERVES 4

Cauliflower is rich in fiber, vitamins and minerals, but can often be somewhat mundane to cook. Until now, that is! Breaking down the head into small florets, coating them with seasoning and roasting them creates crisp and caramelized bites that can be served as a side dish or tossed into salads, pasta, used as a topping for hearty soups, or put out as an appetizer (and served with my personal favorite, Sriracha mayo).

1 head cauliflower, washed

Olive oil

Salt and pepper, to taste

Garlic powder

Chili powder

Preheat oven to 375°F. Cut cauliflower into small florets and arrange on a baking sheet. Drizzle with oil and sprinkle with desired amounts of seasoning. Bake until cauliflower is tender and slightly browned.

COOK'S NOTE: To make Sriracha mayo dipping sauce, combine 1 cup of mayo and 3 tablespoons Sriracha. For a spicier dip, add more hot sauce, to taste.

Stuffed Cabbage

SERVES 6

One of my favorite comfort foods, while time consuming to make, the end result is most definitely worth it. These bundles are filled with flavor!

1 head green cabbage

1½ pounds ground beef

Olive oil

1 onion, chopped

1 clove garlic, minced

½ cup cooked rice

2 teaspoons salt

1 teaspoon garlic powder

¼ teaspoons pepper

1 (28-ounce) can tomato sauce

Trim center core out of the cabbage and submerge head into boiling water for 5 minutes. Drain cabbage and carefully pull off 16 to 18 of the largest outer leaves. Trim off the thick ribs, if any.

Meanwhile, heat olive oil in a large skillet. Add ground beef and brown. Add onion and garlic and cook until softened. Remove from heat and add cooked rice, seasonings, and half of the can of tomato sauce.

Put a heaping tablespoon of prepared filling in the center of each cabbage leaf. Roll up and tuck in the ends, making a package. Spread a small amount of tomato sauce on the bottom of a shallow metal or glass baking dish. Place cabbage rolls side by side in dish and top with remaining sauce. Cheese can also top rolls if desired. Cover and bake in a preheated 350°F oven for 45 to 60 minutes.

Pear Crumble

Sliced almonds or walnuts can be used in place of the pecans in this recipe. This dessert is also best served warm with ice cream or whipped cream.

FILLING

4 ripe pears

3 tablespoons sugar

½ teaspoon cinnamon

1 tablespoon lemon juice

TOPPING

¾ cup flour

¾ cup brown sugar

½ cup rolled oats

1 teaspoon cinnamon

¼ teaspoon nutmeg

¼ teaspoon salt

½ cup butter, softened and cubed

½ cup chopped pecans

Preheat oven to 350°F. Grease the bottom and sides of an 8 x 8-inch baking dish.

For the filling, cut the stem and bottom of each pear and peel. Slice each pear in half and using a spoon, remove the inside spine and the seeds. Chop the pears into medium-sized chunks and place in prepared baking dish. Top with sugar, cinnamon, and lemon juice, and toss.

For the topping, whisk flour, brown sugar, oats, cinnamon, nutmeg, and salt. Add the butter and combine with a fork or pastry blender until butter is the size of peas. Combine the pecans.

Add a third of the topping mixture to the pears and toss. Sprinkle the remaining topping on top. Bake until bubbly and browned, 40 to 45 minutes. Remove from oven and allow to cool for 20 minutes before serving.

Bourbon Maple Apple Cake

SERVES 8

This recipe includes several comforting and warming fall flavors that combine to make a perfect dessert. Any variety of apple can be used, but a darker maple syrup is recommended for a deeper flavor.

CAKE

1½ cups flour

1 teaspoon baking soda

1 teaspoon cinnamon

½ teaspoon nutmeg

½ teaspoon ground ginger

½ teaspoon salt

¾ cup butter, melted and cooled

2 eggs

¼ cup pure maple syrup

¾ cup brown sugar

1 apple, peeled, cored, and grated

APPLES

2 medium apples, peeled, cored, and sliced

½ cup pure maple syrup

4 tablespoons butter

½ cup brown sugar

¼ teaspoon cinnamon

¼ teaspoon nutmeg

½ cup bourbon

Preheat oven to 350°F. Grease the bottom and sides of a 9-inch round cake pan. Arrange the apples in the bottom of the prepared cake pan in a circle to cover.

In a medium saucepan over medium-high heat, combine the maple syrup, butter, brown sugar, cinnamon and nutmeg. Heat until the butter melt and the mixture begins to bubble, about 4 minutes. Remove from heat and stir in bourbon. Pour half the mixture over the apples in the pan. Reserve the remaining mixture to pour over the cake after cooked.

For the cake, whisk flour, baking soda, cinnamon, nutmeg, ginger, and salt. In a separate bowl, combine melted butter, eggs, maple syrup, brown sugar, and grated apple. Add the apple mixture to the flour mixture and mix well. Spoon batter over apples in the pan and smooth the top.

Bake cake until pick inserted in the center of the cake comes out clean, 40 to 50 minutes. Let cool for 5 minutes. Run a knife along the edges to loosen and invert onto a serving plate. Drizzle cake with remaining syrup mixture and let cool slightly before serving.

Pork Chops with Apples & Cabbage

SERVES 5

Deglazing the pan with ginger beer after cooking the pork chops adds a surprising flavor that compliments the tartness of the apples, as well as accenting with the fresh ginger in the dish.

3 teaspoons salt

2 teaspoons pepper

2 teaspoons garlic powder

1 cup flour

5 pork chops

Olive oil

1 can ginger beer

1 onion, thinly sliced

1 small head cabbage, coarsely chopped

1 large apple, peeled and sliced

2 teaspoons freshly grated ginger

Season both sides of chops with salt, pepper, and garlic powder. Dredge in flour. Heat oil in a large skillet and brown chops on both sides. When browned, remove chops and set aside. Deglaze pan with half can of ginger beer, scraping bits off the bottom of the pan.

Add onion to pan and cook until tender. Add cabbage and apples to pan, cover, and cook until cabbage is wilted, about 15 minutes, stirring occasionally. Add remainder of ginger beer and grated ginger and cook, covered, another 15 minutes until cabbage is tender.

Add chops back to pan and cook until heated, about 5 minutes more.

SCRUMPY EWE CIDER

WEST FULTON, NY

"TRADITIONAL CIDER, MADE in the foothills of the Catskill Mountains." Scrumpy Ewe Cider is an independently-run New York State Farm Cidery that ferments and grows a variety of European, heirloom and wild seedling apples in the fertile Schoharie Valley. Their dry ciders are a direct result of owner Ryan McGivers's time as a stone mason and touring musician, where he had the privilege of visiting cider producing countries in Europe. He learned what apple varieties were traditionally used to craft the best cider, in some cases for over 300 years.

Everything starts with picking quality cider apples from the orchards. His mother's family, the Von Lindens, have farmed the Schoharie Valley since the early 19th century and he and his brother continue this tradition by growing quality bittersharp and bittersweet cider apples. Whether it is from the fruit they grow at Scrumpy Ewe Orchards, or from the various orchards they work with in areas ranging from the Hudson Valley to the Finger Lakes, all the cider begins with hand-selecting each apple based on its unique characteristics to be used as a standalone single varietal or as part of greater blend.

After the harvest season, the apple bins are transported to Scrumpy Ewe's Facility in Charlotteville, NY. There, everything is washed, from apple to machine. After a thorough cleaning, they grind the apples into pomace and make fresh juice using a commercial bladder press. The discarded apple-bits go back to the Scrumpy Ewes on the farm.

Next, yeast is added to the juice within 48 hours, and primary fermentation begins for a 1 to 3-month period, depending on the size of batch, method of fermentation, and temperature of the room. With certain ciders, they pitch no yeast at all and let the wild, native yeasts do the fermenting. Either way, the juice is monitored as it ferments with temperature gauges, hydrometers and digital meters for PH/total acidity/sulfites (if any are added). Batches are racked off of their lees using oxygen-free wine pumps to ensure no oxidation occurs at any point in the process.

During the secondary fermentation process, the product is aged in either stainless steel tanks and/or American oak barrels for an additional 6 weeks to 16 months, depending. When the ideal time comes, a decision is made to filter the remaining sediment out of the cider or leave it cloudy, depending on the particular batch. The cider is then labeled and hand bottled either still or force carbonated. The cider is allowed to refrigerate for another month before it's ready to be consumed.

The cider shack in West Fulton is on a back road, in what seems to be the middle of nowhere. Thankfully, its yellow sign and white fence make it easy to spot. Hand-done woodworking and natural light make the tasting room a pleasurable atmosphere all its own, ideal for enjoying a glass of cider. Bottles of cider are ready to take home once you figure out your favorite blend.

A true farm to table establishment, Scrumpy Ewe also offers a variety of workshops throughout the year, teaching everything from grafting to knitting. Small, intimate musical concerts with small plate food offerings are also frequent, featuring talented musicians as well as skilled chefs, bringing the community together.

Hard Cider Braised Pork Tacos

SERVES 8

The Stone Cutter hard cider provides strong notes of acidity as compared to other hard ciders. The cider is also very dry as opposed to sweet, so that it is not overwhelming when combined with the pork.

PORK

1 (4 pound) pork butt

1 medium onion, sliced

1 head garlic, smashed

1 teaspoon coriander seeds, toasted

Salt and pepper, to taste

2 cups Scrumpy Ewe Stone Cutter hard cider

PICKLED JALAPEÑOS

1 large jalapeño, sliced

1 cup cider vinegar

½ cup water

1 teaspoon sugar

½ teaspoon salt

½ teaspoon whole peppercorns

½ teaspoon coriander seeds

TOPPINGS

Small corn tortillas

Red leaf lettuce

Cilantro

Avocado

Green onion

Lime

Rinse pork and cut in half. Place in a crockpot, adding sliced onions, smashed garlic, coriander seeds, salt and pepper and cider. Cover and set to high. Cook until pork is tender and is able to be shredded, 7 to 8 hours.

To make quick-pickled jalapeños, combine vinegar, water, sugar, salt, peppercorns and coriander seeds in a small saucepan. Bring mixture to a boil. Place sliced jalapeños in a mason jar and pour hot liquid over them. Let sit at room temperature until ready to use.

When pork is done and shredded, season with more salt and pepper if needed. Remove 2 cups of pork liquid and place in a small saucepan. Cook over high heat to bring the mixture to a rapid boil. Allow mixture to reduce until dark in color and thickened, about 5 minutes. Remove from heat.

To assemble tacos, heat tortilla in a pan on both sides. Transfer to plate and top with shredded pork, lettuce, cilantro, sliced avocado, green onion, pickled jalapeño, reduced sauce and a squeeze of lime juice.

Apple Cider Doughnuts

MAKES 18

Cider doughnuts are probably one of my favorite things about the cooler weather coming into the Catskills. You can eat them plain, but I prefer mine with cinnamon sugar.

Oil for frying

1 cup sugar

5 tablespoons butter, room temperature

2 eggs, room temperature

3½ cups flour, plus more for dusting

1¼ teaspoons salt

2 teaspoons baking powder

1 teaspoon baking soda

1½ teaspoons cinnamon

½ teaspoon nutmeg

½ cup buttermilk

⅓ cup boiled apple cider

1 tablespoon vanilla extract

Cinnamon sugar

In a large bowl using a stand mixer with the whisk attachment, beat sugar and butter until mixture is pale and fluffy, about 4 to 6 minutes. Add eggs one at a time, beating a minute after each addition.

In a medium bowl, whisk together flour, salt, baking powder, baking soda, cinnamon, and nutmeg, set aside. Combine buttermilk, boiled cider, and vanilla into butter mixture and mix well. Add flour mixture and combine just until moistened.

Line two baking sheets with parchment and dust with flour. Pat dough gently into ¾-inch thickness on sheet. Sprinkle dough with flour, cover with plastic wrap and place in freezer for 10 minutes. Remove dough from freezer and, using a floured 3-inch doughnut cutter, cut out 18 doughnuts with holes. Place cut doughnuts on other tray and firm in freezer for 5 minutes. Dough scraps can be rolled out again as needed.

In a Dutch oven, heat 3 inches of oil to 370°F. Drop 3 to 4 doughnuts into oil and cook until browned on one side, about 1 minute, then flip to cook the other side. Repeat with remaining dough and place cooked doughnuts onto a paper towel-lined plate. Sprinkle hot doughnuts with cinnamon sugar and serve immediately.

COOK'S NOTE:

You can prepare the boiled cider by simmering 1½ cups of fresh apple cider down to ⅓ cup in about 25 minutes.

Upside-Down Apple Pie

SERVES 12

There is such a thing as an upside-down cake; why not an upside-down pie? This is a fun, unique take on a classic, adding a sweet, gooey pecan glaze to the "bottom" crust and turning an already-great apple pie into the ultimate autumn indulgence.

GLAZE

¼ cup brown sugar

1 tablespoon butter, melted

1 tablespoon corn syrup

¼ cup pecan halves

CRUST

Pastry for one-crust pie (see page 36 for recipe), doubled

FILLING

⅓ cup sugar

2 tablespoons flour

½ teaspoon cinnamon

4 cups sliced, peeled

In a 9-inch pie pan, combine brown sugar, butter, and corn syrup, and mix well. Spread mixture evenly in bottom of pan and arrange pecans over mixture. Prepare pastry and place bottom pastry over mixture in pan, gently pressing to fit pan.

Preheat oven to 425°F. In a small bowl, combine sugar, flour, and cinnamon; mix well. Arrange half of apple slices in pastry-lined pan; sprinkle with half of sugar mixture. Repeat with remaining apple slices and sugar mixture. Top with remaining pastry. Fold edge of top pastry under bottom pastry and press together to seal edges. Cut several slits in top of pastry.

Bake at 425°F for 8 minutes. Reduce oven temperature to 325°F and bake an additional 25 to 35 minutes, or until crust is golden brown. Loosen edge of pie and carefully invert onto serving plate. Serve warm with vanilla ice cream or whipped cream.

> **COOK'S NOTE:** For the more adventurous, you can do the same thing with a peach pie, which also pairs great with brown sugar and pecans.

Grilled Trout

SERVES 1

There are many places throughout the Catskill Mountains well suited to fishing, especially for trout. Serve this as an appetizer or as a main dish, all depending on how many fish have been caught.

1 whole trout, cleaned

1 shallot, thinly sliced

Fresh parsley

Fresh dill

2 lemon wedges

2 tablespoons butter

Garlic powder

Salt and pepper, to taste

Place trout on a medium-sized piece of aluminum foil. Open inside of trout and season with garlic powder, salt, and pepper. Stuff trout with sliced shallots, fresh herbs, and lemon wedges and butter. Fold foil around prepared trout to create a pouch.

Place trout packet on grill and cook until fish is cooked and flakey.

Mashed Jerusalem Artichokes

SERVES 4

The Jerusalem artichoke, or sunchoke, is considered a root vegetable and grows abundantly in the Northeast. It has absolutely nothing in common with the artichoke however, and should be thought of more as a potato. With a very mild flavor, low calorie count, and high fiber content, they are the perfect low carb side to pair with wild game like venison or duck.

6-8 Jerusalem artichokes, washed

4 tablespoons butter

½ cup fresh parsley, chopped

Juice of half a lemon

Salt and pepper, to taste

Bring a pot of salted water to a boil. Peel and chop washed artichokes into medium chunks. Boil until tender, then drain and mash until smooth. Add butter, parsley, juice of half a lemon, and salt and pepper to taste.

Farrow with White Beans & Kale

SERVES 4

This dish can be served as a side dish, but is also hearty enough to be a vegetarian main course if you swap out the chicken stock for vegetable.

1 cup dry farro

3 cups chicken stock
(see page 192 for recipe)

1 (15-ounce) can white
beans, rinsed

1 bay leaf

½ cup Gruyère cheese,
shredded

3 tablespoons grated
Parmesan cheese

4 teaspoons olive oil

8 ounces baby Bella
mushrooms, sliced

¼ cup shallots, thinly sliced

3 cloves garlic, minced

4 cups chopped kale

½ teaspoon salt

½ teaspoon pepper

2 tablespoons chopped
fresh parsley

In a medium saucepan, bring farro, stock, and bay leaf to a boil over medium-high heat. Reduce heat to medium-low and let simmer until grains are tender but still chewy, about 30 minutes.

Stir beans into hot grains. Add cheeses and stir until melted. Cover and keep warm. Meanwhile, in a medium skillet, heat 2 teaspoons olive oil over medium-high heat. Add mushrooms and cook until browned on both sides, about 6 to 8 minutes. Transfer to a bowl.

Add the remaining olive oil to skillet and cook shallots and garlic, stirring, about 30 seconds. Add the kale and cook, stirring frequently, until wilted, about 3 minutes. Season with salt and pepper. Stir the kale, mushrooms, and parsley into the farro and serve.

Savory Squash Bread Pudding

SERVES 8

A decadent take on a normally sweet dish, this recipe could also be used in place of stuffing for a Thanksgiving dinner.

4 tablespoons butter

12 cups brioche, cut into 1-inch pieces

1 small butternut squash, peeled, seeds removed, cut into ½-inch pieces

2 large leeks, white and pale green parts only, halved lengthwise, cut into ½-inch pieces

1 teaspoon fresh thyme

2 teaspoons salt

4 large eggs

3 cups heavy cream

3 cups whole milk

1 teaspoon sugar

Cayenne pepper

1½ cups grated Gouda, divided

Preheat oven to 350°F. Butter a 13 x 9-inch glass or ceramic baking dish and set aside. Spread out brioche on a large baking sheet and bake, tossing halfway through, until golden brown and crisp, 25 to 30 minutes. Let cool, then transfer to a large bowl.

Heat remaining butter in a large skillet over medium heat. Cook squash, leeks, and thyme, stirring occasionally until squash is tender, 10 to 12 minutes. Mix in a pinch of cayenne and season with salt. Transfer to bowl with brioche.

Whisk eggs, cream, milk, sugar, salt, and a pinch of cayenne in a large bowl to combine. Add 1 cup cheese to bowl with brioche and toss to evenly distribute. Transfer to prepared baking dish and pour 5 cups egg mixture over. Gently press bread into liquid to coat. Pour remaining egg mixture over and let sit 15 minutes.

Scatter remaining ½ cup cheese over bread pudding and bake until puffed and custard is set in the center, 60 to 75 minutes. Let cool at least 10 minutes before serving.

Bourbon Brined Turkey with Pan Gravy

SERVES 10

Brining is the best way to prepare a turkey, both because of the flavor and the moist results. I use a 12-15 pound turkey, but the recipe can easily be increased in order to accommodate a larger bird. I also recommend using a darker grade of maple syrup for a richer taste.

BRINE

16 cups cold water

¾ cup salt

¾ cup pure maple syrup

¾ cup bourbon

4 fresh thyme sprigs

6 fresh sage leaves

TURKEY

1 whole turkey, 12–15 pounds, thawed, neck and giblets removed

2 onions, cut into wedges

4 tablespoons butter, softened

Fresh thyme and sage

Salt and pepper, to taste

Garlic powder

GLAZE

½ cup orange juice

½ cup pure maple syrup

1 tablespoon Dijon mustard

½ teaspoon salt

2 tablespoons bourbon

GRAVY

Pan drippings

¼ cup bourbon

4-5 cups chicken stock

¼ cup cold water

4 tablespoons cornstarch

Salt and pepper

2 tablespoons fresh thyme, chopped

For brine, in a large saucepan, heat 3 cups water, ¾ cup salt, ¾ cup maple syrup, ¾ cup bourbon, thyme and sage to simmering over medium heat. Cook and stir until salt is dissolved, about 6 minutes. Pour into large stockpot (noncorrosive) and let cool to room temperature, about 20 minutes. Add remaining 13 cups cold water.

Add turkey to brine mixture. If brine does not cover turkey, add more water. Cover and refrigerate 8 to 12 hours, turning once.

Preheat oven to 325°F. Remove bird from brine, and rinse inside and out with cold water. Discard brine. Place bird breast-side up on roasting rack inside roasting pan, and pat dry with paper towels. Place onion

continued on the next page

inside turkey's cavity. Tuck wings underneath bird, coat skin with butter and season with salt, pepper, and garlic powder, as well as fresh herbs. Roast turkey for 3 hours to 3 hours 45 minutes.

Meanwhile, make glaze by combining orange juice, ½ cup maple syrup, mustard and ½ teaspoon salt in medium saucepan over medium heat, beating with a whisk. Bring to a simmer and cook 10 to 13 minutes, stirring occasionally, until thickened and reduced by about one-third.

Remove from heat; stir in bourbon. Set aside. In last 30 minutes of roasting, brush turkey with half of the glaze, then roast about 15 more minutes. Brush turkey with remaining glaze and roast about 15 minutes longer or until skin is deep mahogany, an instant-read thermometer inserted into the thickest part of thigh reads 165°F, and drumsticks move easily when lifted or twisted. Let turkey rest, loosely covered with foil, 15 minutes before carving.

To make gravy, remove turkey from roasting pan. Place pan on burners on medium-high heat. Scrape up browned bits and add bourbon and cook until almost evaporated. Add chicken stock and bring to a boil. Combine the cold water and cornstarch and whisk into pan. Continue whisking until gravy thickens. Add salt and pepper to taste and fresh thyme. Serve.

Two Potato Gratin

SERVES 8

This dish combines two Thanksgiving favorites—white potatoes and sweet potatoes—and coats them with a rich and creamy cheese sauce.

3 pounds mixed russet potatoes and sweet potatoes

Butter for baking dish and foil

1½ cups heavy whipping cream

½ cup chicken broth (see page 192 for recipe)

1 tablespoon chopped sage

1 clove garlic, minced

1 teaspoon salt

Pepper, to taste

1 cup grated Gruyère cheese

Spread potatoes in a buttered 11 x 7-inch baking dish. Combine heavy cream, chicken broth, chopped sage, garlic, and salt and pour over potatoes. Sprinkle with pepper. Cover with buttered foil and bake at 425°F for 35 minutes. Sprinkle with cheese. Bake uncovered until brown and bubbling, about 25 minutes. Let rest before serving.

Roasted Brussels Sprouts

SERVES 6

Brussels sprouts are among those vegetable that people tend to shy away from, all because they think they don't like them. And that's because they've never had roasted Brussels sprouts! Boiled or steamed Brussels sprouts are nowhere near as delicious as roasted Brussels sprouts, which combine a mildly bitter flavor with a slight crispness from the oven, all topped off with fresh lemon juice that makes for a hearty side to any late fall dinner or even as a healthy snack.

1½ pounds trimmed
   Brussels sprouts

Olive oil

Salt and pepper, to taste

Lemon zest

Preheat oven to 400°F. Slice sprouts in half. Place trimmed and sliced Brussels sprouts on a baking sheet. Drizzle with olive oil to coat, and season with salt and pepper.

Roast for 30 to 45 minutes, turning every 5 to 7 minutes to allow even browning. Serve with fresh lemon zest.

COOK'S NOTE: You can cook the Brussels sprouts in a large cast iron skillet for easy serving.

Bourbon Spiced Pumpkin Pie

SERVES 8

You cannot go through the entire fall season without making at least one pumpkin pie. This recipe combines all of the warming spices that are welcomed in the autumn as well as the faint hint of bourbon, which brings out the spices even more.

Pastry for one-crust pie
  (see page 36 for recipe)

1½ cups pureed pumpkin

1 cup sugar

1 tablespoon brown sugar

1 cup heavy cream

3 eggs

2 tablespoons bourbon

1 teaspoon cinnamon

1 teaspoon nutmeg

½ teaspoon ginger

½ teaspoon salt

½ teaspoon pumpkin pie
  spice

In a large mixing bowl, combine the pumpkin, sugars and cream and mix well. Add eggs, one at a time, until the mixture is well blended. Add the bourbon and spices and stir until blended, making sure there are no lumps.

Line a 9-inch pie pan with the prepared pastry, and crimp edges. Pour in pumpkin filling. Brush pastry with milk or egg white. Bake in an oven preheated to 450°F for 10 minutes. Lower oven temperature to 300°F and bake pie for another 45–50 minutes, or until firm. Cool and serve with whipped cream.

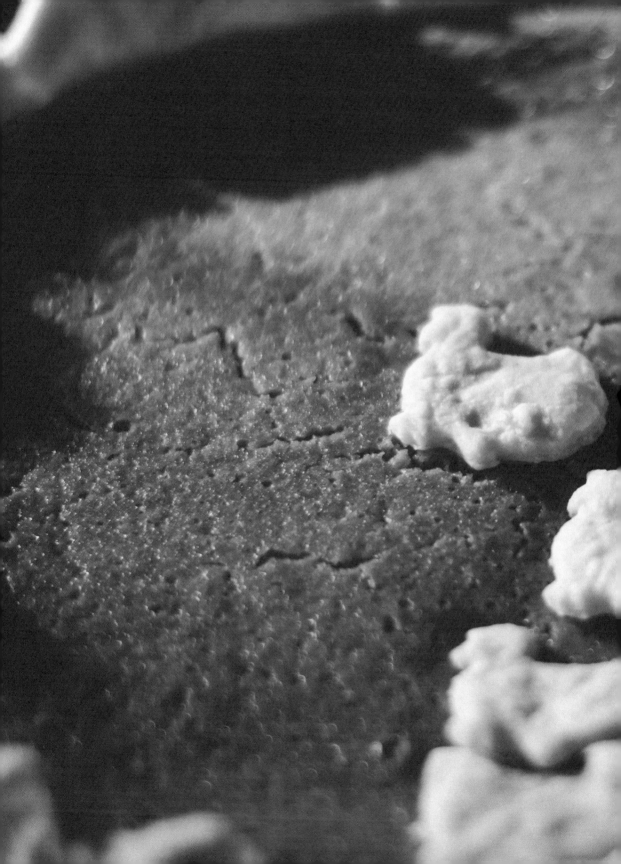

Honey Sage Bourbon Cocktail

MAKES 2

While honey is available year round, it's actually harvested from the hives in the fall, after everything is done blooming but before the winter months. Both honey and sage have their own distinct flavor, but reducing the two in a simple syrup melds them perfectly.

HONEY SAGE SYRUP

1 cup water

½ cup honey

10 fresh sage leaves

COCKTAIL

3 ounces bourbon

3 tablespoons honey sage syrup

1 orange peel

1 fresh sage leaf

To make the syrup, bring the water, honey, and sage to a boil in a pot over medium high heat. Reduce to low and simmer for 3 minutes. Turn off heat and let syrup cool.

Stir bourbon and cooled syrup with ice in a mixing glass. Fill rocks glass with ice and pour mix over. Twist orange peel directly over glass to release oils. Garnish with a fresh sage leaf.

COOK'S NOTE: The syrup can be stored in the fridge for up to two weeks and used as needed.

Winter

Kale Pesto

MAKES ABOUT 2 CUPS

The hardy kale always seems to hold on the longest in the garden, lasting even past the first snowfall. In this recipe, we're using kale in place of basil and having walnuts replace the pine nuts you'd usually see in this type of pesto. I grow both Tuscan (flat leaf) and curly leaf kale in my garden, so I can attest that either works well (a mixture of both is another option). Serve mixed in with pasta, potatoes, scrambled eggs, or as a spread for sandwiches and grilled cheese.

5 cloves garlic

6-8 kale stalks, chopped

Olive oil

½ cup walnuts

¼ cup Parmesan cheese

Salt and pepper, to taste

Puree the garlic and kale, adding olive oil a little at a time to form a loose paste. Add walnuts and cheese and blend, allowing walnuts to be finely chopped. Season with salt and pepper to taste.

> **COOK'S NOTE:** Unlike with other pesto recipes, it's been my experience that kale does not freeze as well. If you make a larger batch, store in the fridge for no more than a week.

Mashed Winter Squash

SERVES 6

Any variety of winter squash can be used in this recipe, thanks to their versatility and availability. Squash is technically harvested in the late fall before being stored in a cool (not freezing), dry place, but certain hearty varieties like acorn, butternut, and Hubbard squash, to name a few, can last through mid-winter, providing fresh squash during even the colder months.

1 large winter squash, any variety

1 teaspoon cinnamon

Salt and pepper, to taste

Garlic powder

¼ cup pure dark maple syrup

3 tablespoons butter

Preheat oven to 475°F. Wash the outside of the squash and slice in half. Remove seeds and place in a large glass or metal baking dish. Add 1 cup of water to the dish. Sprinkle squash with cinnamon, salt, pepper, and garlic powder. Bake squash until tender.

Scoop baked squash into serving bowl and add maple syrup and butter. Mash until smooth and combined. Season with more salt and pepper if needed.

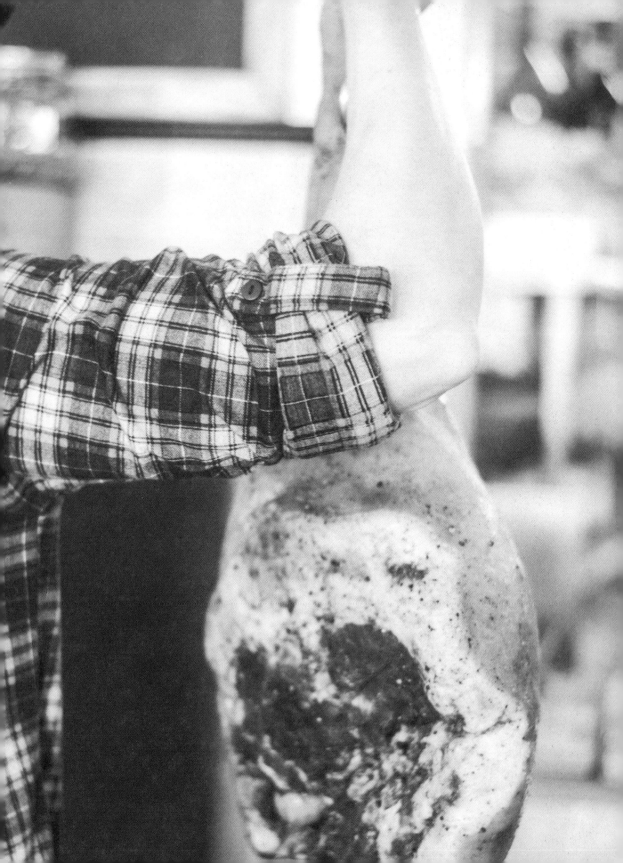

SOLINSKY'S

STAMFORD, NY

Solinsky's Smokehouse is a dream long in the making, brought true by owners Caitlan Grady and Michael Solyn, who both have a passion for local, traditionally processed foods.

Michael, a graduate of the Culinary Institute of America, is the latest of many generations in the food industry. His great grandparents owned a delicatessen in Youngstown, Ohio. When it closed during World War II, his grandfather and namesake, Myron, took a job in the steel industry. But Myron kept his dream of great food alive while eating Limburger, raw onion, and pumpernickel sandwiches. On the other side of his family, Mike's maternal grandparents owned a large seafood business in Atlantic City, NJ, and his mother was an enthusiastic amateur cook, taking classes to supplement her passion.

Caitlan's mother's family has deep roots in central New York, acting as avid outdoor enthusiasts, naturalists, and foragers. Her father, hailing from Staten Island, instilled in her a love for raw shellfish, snappy hot dogs, and international foods of all kinds.

When Caitlan and Michael began working together on catering jobs in NYC, both already had a dream to move to the Catskills and open a locally sourcing

USDA processing facility. They moved back to the Catskills in 2010 and produced their first line of product. To this day you can see the "Wedding Ham," made in 2010, hanging in their store.

With the incredible land and the vast amount of forage, soft and hard mast, and sweet mineral grass available, the Catskill region produces incredible quality animals. This quality is the foundation of Solinsky's and the dream to make the finest Salumi and smoked meat products to rival any in the world.

The experience at Solinsky's is an ode to the past. Customers are transported back in time to their grandparent's local meat shop, with delicious smokey smells, hanging meats, and service by name. Always quick with a sample of what's in the case or a new project being worked on, they strive to give visitors an incredible experience that is delicious and personal. Food is a vehicle for love, and Solinsky's has lots to give.

Catskill Carbonara

SERVES 6

Though similar dishes have existed in Italy for at least 200 years, pasta a la carbonara is most likely a product of post-World War II. It is said American officers stationed around Rome provided bacon and eggs to the locals and enjoyed this dish very much. Born from making something filling, delicious, and simple from what you have in the pantry or can find locally, feel free to use pancetta, guanciale, or smoked bacon in your rendition. Remember: there are few ingredients, so use the best eggs, cheese, and pork you can get, and of course fresh cracked pepper.

Salt

2 large eggs, plus 2 large yolks, room temperature

2 ounces (about 2/3 packed cup) grated hard cheese, plus additional for serving

Coarsely ground black pepper, to taste

1 tablespoon olive oil

4 ounces of pancetta or guanciale

8-12 ounces spaghetti or your favorite dried pasta

Reserved pasta water

Place a large pot of lightly salted water over high heat and bring to a boil. Fill a large bowl with hot water for serving, and set aside.

In a mixing bowl, whisk together the eggs, yolks and cheese. Season with a pinch of salt and lots of black pepper.

Heat oil in a large skillet over medium heat, add the pork, and sauté until the fat renders. Remove from heat and set aside. The rendered fat and starchy pasta water is the key to a great sauce.

Add pasta to the water and boil until a bit firmer than al dente. Just before pasta is ready, reheat guanciale in skillet, then drain pasta and add to the skillet over low heat. Stir for a minute or so.

Empty serving bowl of hot water, dry it and add hot pasta mixture. Stir in cheese and egg mixture, adding some reserved pasta water if needed for creaminess. Serve immediately, dressing it with grated cheese and pepper.

Venison Tenderloin with Mushrooms

SERVES 4

A hefty amount of various mushrooms help to create a hearty sauce to accompany these tender medallions of venison loin. This comforting dish is best served over egg noodles.

4 venison loins

4 tablespoons butter

1 onion, chopped

2 cups mushrooms, sliced

3 cups chicken stock
(see page 192 for recipe)

¼ cup fresh parsley,
chopped

Salt and pepper, to taste

Garlic powder

Melt butter in a large skillet. Add onion and cook until tender. Cut tenderloin into ½ to ¾-inch medallions. Add to pan and cook until cooked through. Add mushrooms and stir. Add chicken stock and simmer until a gravy has formed, about 15 minutes. Add parsley and season with salt, pepper and garlic powder.

Venison Chili

SERVES 6

A mix of ground beef and ground venison can be used in this recipe, or just beef. This chili is not mild, but rather hot when it comes to flavor, and is best served over rice.

1 pound ground venison

2 tablespoons olive oil

1 green bell pepper, chopped

1 large onion, chopped

2 cloves garlic, minced

1 small jalapeño, minced

1 (28-ounce) can crushed tomatoes

1 can kidney beans, drained

2 tablespoons chili powder

1 teaspoon cumin

1 teaspoon dried oregano

1 teaspoon cayenne powder

1 teaspoon salt

1 teaspoon pepper

½ teaspoon garlic powder

In a large Dutch oven, heat olive oil over medium heat. Add venison and brown. Add the bell pepper, onion, garlic, and jalapeño and cook until tender. Add the tomatoes and seasonings and stir. Cover, reduce heat, and cook for 4 hours.

Add the beans during the last half hour of cooking. Adjust seasoning if needed.

Smoked Ham & Pea Soup

SERVES 4-6

The best part of this soup is that it utilizes the bones as well as the meat to help create a rich and hearty flavor. Great as a starter to a meal, or as the main dish.

1 cup dry split peas

4 cups chicken stock
(see page 192 for recipe)

1½ pounds smoked meaty
ham bone

¼ teaspoon dried
marjoram

1 bay leaf

½ cup carrot, chopped

½ cup celery, chopped

½ cup onion, chopped

Salt and pepper, to taste

Rinse peas. In a stockpot, combine peas, stock, meat, marjoram, bay leaf, and pepper. Bring to a boil. Reduce heat, cover, and simmer for 1 hour, stirring occasionally. Remove meat. Cut meat off bone and coarsely chop. Return meat to pot. Stir in carrot, celery, and onion. Return to a boil and reduce heat. Cover and simmer for 20 to 30 minutes or until vegetables are tender.

Chicken Stock

MAKES ABOUT 4 QUARTS

A good stock is the base for almost all soups, and is the best way to utilize a chicken carcass after a roast chicken dinner. Stock is different from broth as it is made mostly from the bones, not meat. It also has a richer flavor from the gelatin released from the bones. The ends of asparagus are not essential but add extra flavor to the stock and are easy to save in the freezer.

Carcass of 1 roasted chicken

1 onion, chopped

4 celery stalks, chopped

3 carrots, chopped

1 cup asparagus ends

1 tablespoon peppercorns

3 sprigs thyme

8 sprigs parsley

3 sage leaves

2 bay leaves

6 quarts cold water

Combine the carcass with all the ingredients in a large stockpot. Cover the chicken with water; note that more may be needed to fully cover it. Bring to a boil, cover, then reduce heat and allow to simmer. Cook stock for 12 to 14 hours, adding more water if needed, to keep chicken submerged. Remove the foam that forms at the top of the stock.

Strain the stock, discarding the solids, then pour into jars that can be stored, refrigerated, or kept in the freezer for up to 6 months.

Cream of Broccoli Soup

SERVES 6

This soup is a great and delicious way to be sure you get your daily serving of vegetables.

1½ pounds broccoli, cut into florets

1 onion, sliced

4 cloves garlic, minced

Olive oil

1 teaspoon salt

1 bay leaf

1 large potato, peeled and diced

4 cups chicken stock (see page 192 for recipe)

¼ teaspoon pepper

1 cup milk

½ cup Parmesan cheese, grated

Steam broccoli until fork tender. In a medium stockpot, heat oil over medium-high heat. Cook onions until tender. Add garlic and cook until slightly browned. Place steamed broccoli in stockpot. Add salt, bay leaf, potato, stock, and pepper, and bring to a boil. Reduce heat to medium, cover, and simmer 15 minutes.

Remove bay leaf. Add milk and simmer for 5 minutes more. Add half the grated cheese and stir to blend. Add more salt and pepper if needed.

With immersion blender, puree the soup. Garnish soup with remaining cheese and serve.

PHOENICIA DINER

PHOENICIA, NY

THE PHOENICIA DINER serves farm-to-counter food to visitors and locals alike in the heart of the Catskills. The Diner provides their own take on traditional favorites made whenever possible, with seasonal and sustainable ingredients sourced from the Catskills and the nearby Hudson Valley's verdant fields. Surrounded by the Catskill Mountains and their natural splendor, they celebrate the distinctly American recreation and leisure their environs offer.

Built in 1962, the Diner was originally located in Long Island, NY until the early 80s, when it was moved to Phoenicia, NY and where it has been operated for over 30 years. Mike Cioffi, who bought the diner in 2012, renovated Phoenicia to stay true to the building's original aesthetic and honor the legacy of the great American Diner.

The rise of the American diner is something that lives on in the collective memory of our culture. The Phoenicia Diner embraces that nostalgia to create a familiar, warm, and inviting dining experience for its customers. It was redesigned to express both the Diner's origins in the 1960s and its progress since, with a bit of fun and kitsch thrown in.

The design, aesthetic, menu, ingredients, and overall feeling of the Diner is inspired by the surrounding environment, and aims to be a genuine representation of the Catskills and all the unique experiences they have to offer.

Together, the Catskills and Hudson Valley host over 5,000 farms built on over 890,000 acres. The Phoenicia Diner makes full use of those agricultural resources and products whenever practical and available, obtaining the majority of their ingredients from local farmers and vendors, and have staff that communicate this connection to their customers knowledgeably and without pretension. From the mixers in their cocktails, to the ice cream in the shakes and the chocolate in the cookies, all are sourced locally.

Because of this, the diner is a community place, drawing a wide range of people from near and far. If a customer takes a look on the board above the kitchen, or on the printed menu, it's easy for them to see that the Phoenicia Diner isn't a typical diner, and because of this, crowds line up for the food.

PHOENICIA
DINER

Puff Pancake for One

SERVES 1

Many of the dishes at the Phoenicia Diner are presented in a single serve cast iron skillet. This puff pancake is super simple, featuring farm fresh eggs and milk, and can be topped with fresh fruit, pure maple syrup and cream…or anything, really!

2 tablespoons butter, plus additional for greasing skillet

1 large egg, beaten

¼ cup milk

¼ teaspoon vanilla

¼ cup all-purpose flour

¼ teaspoon nutmeg

Preheat oven to 475°F. In a small bowl, whisk all ingredients together.

Place butter in a 5-inch cast iron skillet. Melt butter in the skillet in the preheated oven. Remove skillet with melted butter and pour in egg mixture. Return to oven and bake 10–15 minutes until pancake is puffed and golden.

Top with fresh fruit, pure maple syrup, jam, or desired toppings. Enjoy the pancake in the skillet.

Goose au Poivre

SERVES 4

Since my brother Daniel is an avid hunter, different types of wild game are almost always available to me. While this is a wild take on the steak version, the goose can also be substituted with venison loin or duck breast.

2 wild goose breasts, cleaned

Salt and pepper, to taste

4 tablespoons butter

1 onion, diced

½ cup chicken stock (see page192 for recipe)

2 tablespoon roughly cracked peppercorns

⅓ cup marsala

¼ cup heavy cream

Slice goose breasts in half and season with salt and pepper. Heat 2 tablespoons butter in a large sauté pan set over medium-high heat. Sear goose, turning only once until done to individual liking. Place cooked goose on cutting board to rest.

Add onion to sauté pan and cook for 2 minutes. Add stock and peppercorns and bring to a boil. Boil down by half. Add marsala and bring back to a boil until thickened, 2 to 4 minutes. Turn off heat and add cream and 2 tablespoons butter. Serve over cooked goose.

Chicken Liver Pâté

SERVES 8

The livers saved from butchering chickens in the early fall are featured in this rich and distinctly flavorful appetizer that is sure to bring a touch of elegance to any gathering.

¾ cup butter

1 cup onion, finely chopped

1 clove garlic, minced

1 teaspoon fresh thyme, minced

¼ teaspoon dried oregano

¼ teaspoon dried sage

¾ teaspoon salt

¼ teaspoon pepper

⅛ teaspoon ground allspice

1 pound chicken livers, trimmed

2 tablespoons bourbon

Melt 1 stick butter in a large skillet over low heat. Cook onion and garlic, stirring until softened, about 5 minutes. Add herbs, salt, pepper, allspice and livers and cook, stirring, until livers are cooked on the outside but still pink on the inside, about 8 minutes. Stir in bourbon and remove from heat. Puree mixture in a food processor until smooth. Transfer to a crock and smooth top.

Melt remaining ½ stick butter in small saucepan over low heat. Remove pan from heat and let stand 3 minutes. Place sprig of fresh thyme on top of pâté. Skim froth from butter and spoon clarified butter over pâté to cover surface.

Chill pâté until butter is firm, about 30 minutes. Cover with plastic wrap and chill at least 2 hours more. Once butter has been broken, pâté can be kept for 1 week (2 weeks without the butter being broken).

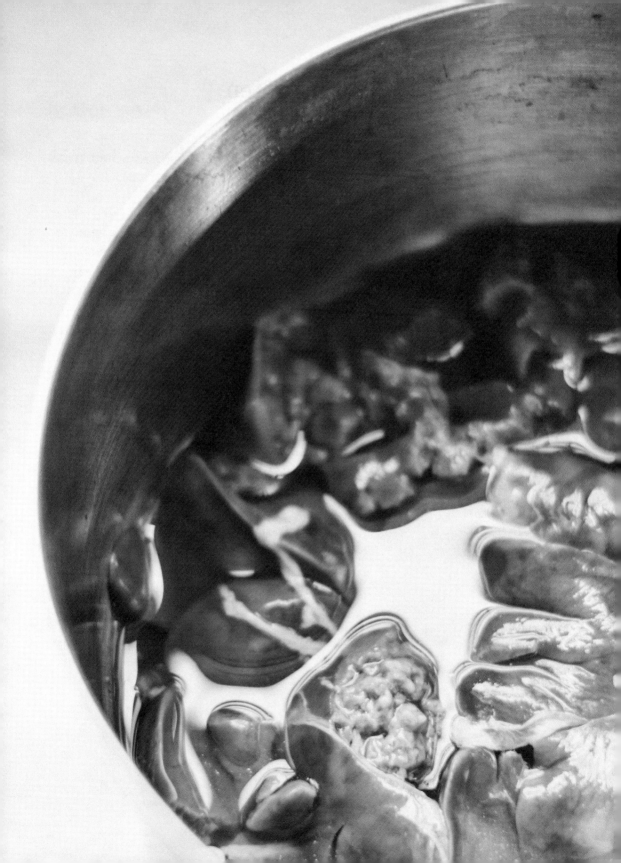

Sauerbraten

SERVES 8

The roast should be marinated for at least 2 days before cooking for the best flavor. This German dish is also best served with red cabbage and egg noodles.

1 (4 pound) venison roast

1 cup water

1 cup red wine vinegar

1 large onion, thinly sliced

1 lemon, thinly sliced

10 whole cloves

4 bay leaves

6 peppercorns

2 tablespoons salt

2 tablespoons sugar

12 gingersnaps, crushed

Place the roast in a deep glass or ceramic bowl. Combine the water, vinegar, onion, lemon, cloves, bay leaves, peppercorns, salt, and sugar and pour mixture over roast. If the prepared liquid does not cover meat, add equal parts water and vinegar until fully submerged.

Cover and refrigerate for 2 to 4 days; the longer it marinates, the more intense the flavor. Turn meat occasionally while marinating.

To cook, place roast in a slow cooker. Pour 1 cup marinade into cooker and cover. Cook on low for 6 to 8 hours, until meat is fork-tender. Remove the meat and keep warm.

To make gravy, strain the liquid and return it to the cooker. Stir in crushed gingersnaps, cover, and cook on high for 10 to 15 minute. Slice meat and serve over egg noodles and top with prepared gravy.

Lard

MAKES 2 CUPS

In my opinion, lard (rendered pork fat) makes a pie crust. Having a mason jar of it in the fridge is just a normal thing, especially if you are an avid baker like myself. The cracklings are just an added bonus.

2 pounds leaf lard

½ cup water

To prepare the pork fat, cut away any lean part that may be attached. Clean your cutting board and cut fat into equal1 inch pieces. If pieces are uneven, some will brown before others. Cover and refrigerate for 2 to 4 days; the longer it marinates, the more intense the flavor. Turn meat occasionally while marinating.

Place fat and ½ cup water (just enough to cover the bottom to prevent fat from burning) in a heavy stock pot over medium-high heat. Stir constantly to prevent burning until the fat begins to melt.

Continue stirring, lowering heat if needed to prevent burning. When all the cracklings have browned and floated to the top, remove from heat and carefully strain fat into a heatproof bowl.

Store lard in a clean, dry container, I prefer the old fashioned canning jars that have the glass lid, and keep in the refrigerator.

The Catskills Farm to Table Cookbook

Maple Bourbon Pecan Pie

SERVES 8

One of my favorite pies to make and eat, this boozy take on a classic is filled with toasted pecans and elevated with the warm flavors of maple and bourbon.

Pastry for one-crust pie
(see page 36 for recipe)

4 tablespoons butter

1½ toasted pecans

¾ cup coarsely chopped
pecans

1 cup brown sugar

½ cup dark maple syrup

½ cup dark corn syrup

3 eggs, beaten

3 tablespoons bourbon

½ teaspoon salt

Preheat to 350°F. Place prepared crust into a 9-inch pie pan, crimping the edges, and refrigerate until ready to fill.

In a large saucepan, melt butter over medium-low heat. Remove from heat and whisk in pecans, brown sugar, maple syrup, corn syrup, eggs, bourbon and salt. Pour filling into the prepared crust. Bake until just set in the middle, about 45 minutes. Transfer to a rack to cool completely.

Stuffed Mushrooms

MAKES 24

Stuffed mushrooms are the perfect party appetizer. The sausage can be swapped out for crab meat if desired.

24 large fresh mushrooms

½ pound Italian sausage

¼ cup green onion, sliced

1 clove garlic, minced

2 tablespoons breadcrumbs

2 tablespoons Parmesan cheese

Preheat an oven to 425°F. Wash and dry mushrooms. Remove stems and reserve caps. Chop enough stems to make 1 cup. In a medium skillet, cook stems, sausage, onion, and garlic until cooked. Drain fat. Stir breadcrumbs and cheese into mixture. Spoon crumb mixture into mushroom caps. Arrange mushrooms on a baking sheet and bake in preheated oven for 8 to 10 minutes or until heated through.

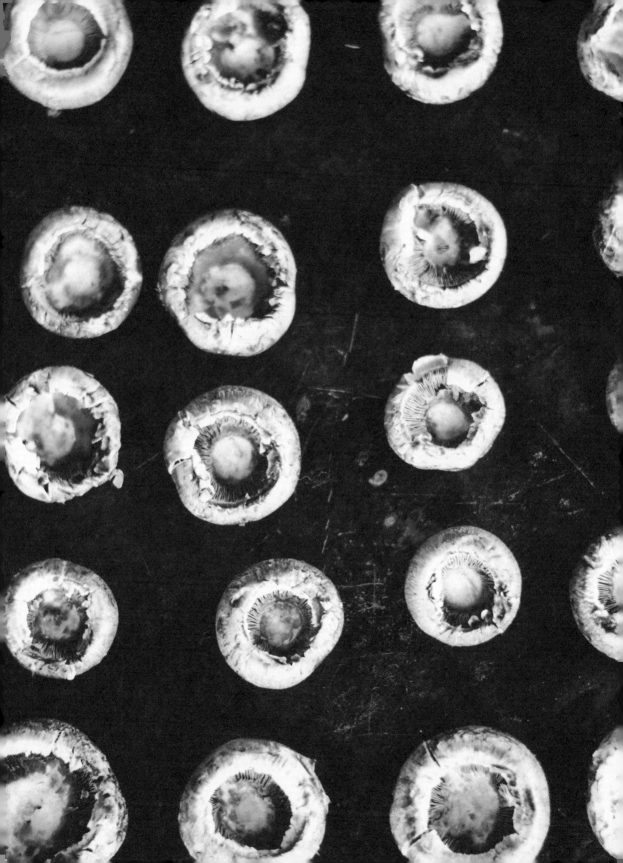

Collard Greens with Bacon

MAKES 24

Collard greens might be the only speck of color left in the garden come winter, depending on the amount of cold weather that hits. Either way, dark greens are typically at local farm stands that are open year round. Kale can also be substituted.

2 bunches collard greens, stemmed

2 tablespoons olive oil

1 medium red onion, thinly sliced

5 slices bacon, cut into 1- inch pieces

1 cup chicken stock (see page 192 for recipe)

2 tablespoons cider vinegar

Black pepper

Working in batches, cut stacked greens through the center, then slice sideways into strips. You can cut them smaller or larger depending on preference. Wash in a colander to remove any grit and dry. In a large skillet, heat oil over medium-high heat. In a large skillet, heat oil over medium-high heat.

Add onion and bacon and cook until onion becomes translucent, about 5 minutes. Add greens and cook until they begin to soften and wilt, being sure to scrape bottom of pan for browned bits. Add chicken stock and reduce heat to allow to simmer and greens become tender, about 12 to 15 minutes. Drizzle with vinegar and season with freshly cracked pepper.

Pork Roast

SERVES 6-8

It's one of the world's great truths: pork roast is best when covered with a savory garlic crust. Pork roast or fresh ham (i.e., ham that isn't smoked) is quite possibly my favorite cut of pork. I find it to be so much more versatile than a smoked ham: the flavor combinations available for both seasonings and side dishes are practically endless. Of course, with all those great options, I still find myself coming back to the garlic crust time and again, but how can you top perfection? Simple to put together and a guaranteed crowd pleaser, this is a great option for get-togethers during the winter holidays.

1 (3 pound) pork roast

2 tablespoons olive oil

5 cloves garlic, minced

Salt and pepper, to taste

1 teaspoon fresh rosemary

Preheat oven to 500°F. In a small bowl, mix the olive oil, garlic, salt and pepper, and rosemary until well combined. Rub over the entire pork roast evenly then place in a roasting pan with the fat side up.

Bake the roast for 15 minutes in the preheated oven, then reduce heat to 325°F. Continue roasting for about 45 minutes or until the thermometer reads 150°F. Remove from oven and let it rest for at least 7 to 10 minutes before slicing.

Maple Cheesecake

SERVES 12

Out of all of the maple products and recipes that I have consumed (and there are quite a few), this is hands-down my favorite. The dark maple syrup used in the recipe creates such a great flavor that I could probably eat the whole thing by myself.

CRUST

4 tablespoons butter, melted

1½ cups graham cracker crumbs

½ cup pecans, ground

3 tablespoons brown sugar

CHEESECAKE

2½ (8-ounce) packages cream cheese, softened

½ cup sugar

3 eggs

1 teaspoon vanilla extract

¼ cup flour

¼ teaspoon baking soda

1 cup heavy cream

1 cup dark pure maple syrup

For crust, combine butter, graham cracker crumbs, ground pecans and brown sugar in a small bowl, and press into the bottom and sides of a 9-inch springform pan.

Preheat oven to 350°F. In a large bowl, beat cream cheese until light and fluffy. Beat in sugar and eggs, one at a time. Beat in vanilla. In a small bowl, stir together flour and baking soda. Add to cream cheese mixture, mixing well. Mix in cream and maple syrup and spoon mixture into springform pan.

Bake until firm, about an hour, or until a toothpick inserted into center comes out clean. Cool on a rack for 30 minutes. Refrigerate. Remove the sides of the springform pan after the cake has been cooled.

COOK'S NOTE: Use a food processor to grind pecans until they resemble the size of the graham cracker crumbs.

Maple Whiskey Sour

MAKES 1

A good whiskey sour is my favorite mixed drink, and adding maple syrup just makes it that much better. Here, maple syrup is being used as a substitute for a simple syrup, which is what balances out the tartness of the lemon juice. It is an absolute must that you use pure maple syrup for the full effect of this recipe, but don't worry: pure maple syrup is available in the Catskills year-round, so be sure to shop local!

2 ounces bourbon

¾ ounce fresh lemon juice

¾ ounce pure maple syrup

Ice

Maraschino cherry and
   orange slice

Add bourbon, lemon juice, maple syrup and ice to a cocktail shaker and vigorously shake for 15 to 20 seconds until sides of shaker are chilled. Strain into a rocks glass with ice and garnish with cherry, orange slice and a dash of cherry juice if desired. Serve.

A Few Final Words

I REALLY DIDN'T THINK creating this cookbook would be as involved as it turned out to be.

Designing, writing, cooking and photographing is intensive, certainly, but most times it is typically only myself doing those things. But when it was decided to add the stories of farms, eateries and businesses involved in the farm to table movement in the Catskills, the workload more than doubled. I methodically wrote down a list of places that I thought would fit the bill, got in contact with them all, began setting up meetings and times for photoshoots, which might then need to be rescheduled due to weather or last-minute unavailability… There were so many components to this aspect of the book (photos, write-ups, recipe collaboration) that I found myself filling in the missing pieces up until the day my first manuscript was due.

But this aspect was easily the best part about creating this book.

Riding on the fender of a John Deere collecting sap, and then watching it boil into syrup until 1 am at Buck Hill Farm; walking through the warm greenhouses at Barbers' with the outside temperature only in the 30s; meeting the chef and manager at the Phoenicia Diner, while photographing (and eating) three plates of food and a milkshake; drinking really good coffee while taking photos of pancetta and enjoying great conversation at Solinsky's; learning about the hard cider process over a glass at Scrumpy Ewe; wandering through a pasture of dairy cows in my Muck boots after driving through mountains; the woods and open fields of Crystal Valley Farm; enjoying rhubarb Collins' and grilled pork chops after photographing pigs in the pasture at Horton Hill Farm; having the restaurant all to myself as I watched the making of the perfect chicken pie over a glass of wine at the Bull & Garland.

I am beyond grateful to have met so many wonderful people who possess immense knowledge in their chosen industries. I also enjoyed the time spent with the people in the featured businesses that I already knew. Cooking and enjoying good food with good company is a big part of the farm to table movement, and I was given the opportunity to enjoy it to the fullest.

Acknowledgments

I AM SO LUCKY to have parents that raised me to appreciate where my food comes from, because if they hadn't instilled in that me, I wouldn't have written a cookbook about it.

Thank you to my friends and family who gave me ideas for recipes and places to feature.

Thank you to all the farms, restaurants, and businesses who are featured in this book. You are a huge aspect of this movement, as well as a big part of this wonderful place that we live in.

About the Author

Courtney Wade is a graphic designer and photographer living in the Catskills Mountain region of New York with an intense passion for good food. With both a degree in graphic design and agricultural business from the State University at Cobleskill, she understands the importance of supporting local producers by purchasing seasonally grown products.

Index